D0205729

WOMEN AND OTHER ALIENS

DEBBIE NATHAN

WOMEN
AND OTHER ALIENS

Essays from the
U.S.-Mexico Border

Cinco Puntos Press  **El Paso, Texas**

Acknowledgements

Many thanks are due to the publications listed below in which the original version of some of these articles appeared:

"The Eyes of Texas" in *The Village Voice*, September 9, 1986.

"America Don't Want No Angry Men" in *The Texas Observer*, November 20, 1987.

"Irma's Story: The Life of an Illegal Alien" in *The Chicago Reader*, July 6, 1984.

"Abortion Stories on the Border" and "Abortion Abcedarium" in *The Texas Observer*, October 27, 1989.

"Sabat's Fifteen Minutes of Fame" in *The Texas Observer*, July 29, 1988.

"Frontier Violence" in *The Texas Observer*, January 6, 1989.

"Sex, the Devil, and Daycare" and "The Making of a Modern Witch Trial" in *The Village Voice*, September 19, 1987.

"The Ritual Sex Abuse Hoax" in *The Village Voice*, January 12, 1990.

FIRST EDITION

ISBN 0-938317-08-3
Library of Congress Catalog Card Number 90-085078

Photo of Debbie Nathan © 1991 by Richard Baron
Cover and book design by Vicki Trego Hill
Data entry by Susannah Mississippi Byrd
Typesetting by TypeGraphics of Texas, Tyler, Texas
Printed on acid free paper by
McNaughton-Gunn, Inc. of Saline, Michigan

Cinco Puntos Press would like to thank The University of Texas at El Paso Library, Special Collections, for permission to use the photograph on the front cover. The photograph is by Luis Villalobos on assignment for the El Paso Times and is archived in the El Paso Times Collection.

CONTENTS

To my parents

Preface

I don't write monographs about *conquistadores*, or poems about coyotes, or novels about the Wild West. I'm not Hispanic, and I didn't grow up here. So sometimes I'm asked (and sometimes I ask myself) how I ended up living in El Paso, Texas, and writing about the U.S.-Mexico border?

It probably has something to do with other places I've been, starting with Houston. I was born and raised there during the postwar baby boom, when people with dishwater-blonde hair and heavy twangs were flocking in from little East Texas towns. Housing developments sprang up almost overnight out of rice fields, NASA was in the planning, and everybody seemed hurried and ambitious about all the growth and promise of Sunbelt future.

They also seemed very anxious. On my side of town, there was a big John Birch Society chapter, and before that, Minute Women who went to school board meetings to guard their children from pinko teachers and subversive texts. The big stores still had two sets of restrooms and water fountains, and at the neighborhood supper tables, my little girlfriends' mommas and daddies worried endlessly about polio, cooties, niggers, desegregation, miscegenation, Reds and spies. In the same breath they talked about Jews. I was Jewish — short and round, not tall and rawboned, with brown eyes rather than blue, and darkish frizzy hair instead of the blonde straight kind. By Junior High chemistry class, white kids with tight curls were being called "Ammonia" (The formula's NH. Hey, NH — Nigger Head.

Get it??). I thus remember spending my childhood in a state of low-grade terror, of free-floating segregation.

So when I went to Mexico for summer school, right before my fourteenth birthday, the world across the border was a revelation. The first thing I noticed was that the girls looked like me. Boys flocked around the plaza, flirting approvingly, calling us *bajita* and *gordita*, as though these were wonderful attributes rather than sad liabilities. They picked us up, lied about their ages, and we did too. On dates, we wandered through the city plaza or waltzed into movie theaters with subtitled Hollywood features. It seems we were always huddled in the dark spot of some public place, and we were always kissing. In a couple of weeks, I had figured out that much of this attention had to do with the fact that we were *gringa* girls rather than Mexicans. In three weeks I had decided things were more complicated and interesting than that. And in six I was dreaming in Spanish.

I came back to Houston with pierced ears, and the kids said I looked like a beaner whore. So be it. There was a world out there, and to get to it all you had to do was hop on a Greyhound. Or even less: just catch a city bus to another side of Houston, where the stores sold dark ginger pastries shaped like piglets, and *Siempre* magazine, with its racy cartoons that mocked Uncle Sam and the Mexican president.

In the late-Sixties I was itching to leave Houston to find more of this world and to look for the metropole at the center of things. My vision was thoroughly American, and among my friends with similar urges, we had this spoken and unspoken list, topped by New York, Chicago, San Francisco. Then Boston, Washington, possibly Detroit. It had to do with art, music, politics, or preferably all three.

That was awhile ago. I've since sampled lots of cities, and the list has dropped down the map so that it now covers Los Angeles, Atlanta and even Albuquerque and Austin. But it still hasn't reached Brownsville/Matamoros, Tijuana/San Diego, or El Paso/Juarez, where I live now and where most of the pieces in this book are set.

That omission seems odd, and I don't think I'm being sentimental. After all, these days who needs to be near Mexico, or even New York, to dream in another language? Anyone who's lived attentively in this country during the last generation has noticed — and probably been moved by — all the Latin American and other Third World people flocking not just to great cities, but to the burgs and suburbs as well, and even to little farm towns from Texas to Kansas to Wisconsin. They represent a maelstrom of energy, and its eye lies farther down, spread over the line of twin cities divided and joined by the international boundary.

The forces arrayed on the border represent striking opposites. On the North, the opulent United States; to the South, under-developed Mexico. At no other place in the world is the income gap between two countries so pronounced, and the resulting clash feels like the kind that creates tornados, or hurricanes. But if there's a storm brewing, this one has the usual quiet at its center. When you ask people how they like living on the border, for instance, you get a generally placid range of answers. El Paso's native working poor usually shrug and talk about how they'd like to go to L.A. and find better jobs and better money, but they stay because the kinfolk are here. Across the river, their counterparts, recently arrived from the Mexican countryside to a place as teeming as Bombay, say there's a lot more food and work here, even if they do have to live in card-board shacks and worry about their daughters' virtue in the city. Another group of recent arrivals, twin plant executives from the American Midwest, crow smugly: they're charmed that the natives say Please and Thank you and Come back soon and God bless you (in both languages). They feel relieved that you can still send your kids to public schools and expect they'll learn manners if not math. You can even live in an old house near the middle of town, without necessarily being rich or poor. And topping off this great sigh of gratitude is *folklore*: fresh tortillas at the supermarkets, mariachis at the lawn parties, little girls in flamenco dresses dancing innocently on sombreros.

Despite (or maybe in keeping with?) this outward contentment, the border has an eerie, about-to-blow feel to it. Some of what's going on here seems dark and dramatic: this is the first U.S. stop, for instance, for the cocaine and grass Americans hunger for so much these days, and the last one for the guns coveted farther South by both *contras* and guerrillas. The fact that the border is plastered with a veritable alphabet of militarization (USAF, CIA, DEA, DoD, FBI, INS) underscores its larger but not so splashy purpose. The U.S.-Mexico line, after all, is where dollars, notions of empire and concomitant imperial mistrust slow down to get translated into correct political and monetary currencies before heading for Latin

America. And here is also where not just the mind-altering commodities, but also the people displaced by these tumultuous renderings make *their* pit stops on the journey north.

All this goes on beneath the glaring desert sun, but clandestine-ness lends border life a strange, steamy cast. In El Paso, you drive up stylish Mesa Road, past the Danish contemporary furniture store and frozen yogurt emporia, and you feel lawlessness: in the women (probably illegal maids) waiting at the bus stops, in the lovely new homes (some of which house drops for Mexican drugrunners), in the unmarked cars with smoked windows in which you glimpse men in sunglasses and mysterious plainclothes, in the arroyos where someone darts from behind a mesquite and you have no idea *what* they're up to. Looking down from the hills of Scenic Drive, you see poisonous smoke rising toward you from the factories and poor shantytowns of Juarez. People and their exhaust unregulated, out of control, yet in the service of the twin plants, of Progress.

The funny thing about all this lawlessness is that it feels so *lawful* — so much part of business. Traditional border scholarship has stressed this area's remoteness from Washington and Mexico City. The federal capitals' geographic and political isolation from the border is said to have foisted unworkable regulations on us, rules that gum things up so much that *fronterizos* on both sides have simply learned to ignore them. But more and more, late 20th century capitalism *everywhere* is basing its survival and growth on making people work for long hours at rock bottom wages without unions or occupational safety or decent housing or environmental controls — in other words, violating tenets of human decency and dignity whose enactment into reality and statute was part of the historical project of the past century. This spiraling descent into neo-barbarism suggests that to mind their countries' fortunes, both the District of Columbia and the Distrito Federal are beginning to *depend* on the same illegality they used to sniff at when considering the border. Does such a turn-about then mean that life on the lawless *frontera* is actually the avant-garde of our larger cosmopolitan *mañana*?

In keeping with that possibility, most of the stories in this book are about people who are considered outlaws. Yet many of them have become criminals by doing normal, useful things — activities defined as wrong because proscribing them makes them easier to control, and thereby cheaper. Or because — as in the case of daycare teachers or

radical poets — to call blameless people outlaws is to put a bandaid
on unbearable social anxieties.

Most of these stories are also about women. That's partly
because, in exploring the edges of uneasiness that bound such issues
as immigration, family and gender-role changes, I've been struck by
how often this culture's worries about social change get displaced into
phobias about female sexuality. The essays herein about U.S.- born
women highlight this issue. I've tried to convey my sense that, when
it comes to the border, much of what feels fast, energetic and therefore engaging centers around the lives and work of women. During
my first visit to Mexico 25 years ago, it was strictly taboo for them to
wear pants on the street, and poor women never wore them
anywhere. Donning trousers is partly just a way of aping First World
style. But it's also a statement about one's participation in life and
work outside the home, and the fact that Mexican border women
now favor pants as much as dresses shows how much their world
has changed.

A generation ago, they stayed home minding the children while
the men went to the U.S. to pick crops. Or they worked in affluent
border homes as maids. But today, many of these women's daughters
are traveling beyond the border, and often by themselves. Meanwhile, twin plants employ mostly women — a fact that has transformed not just their dress but their stance towards parents, husbands,
boyfriends, children, birth control, housekeeping, wage work and
civic life.

A radical male friend, while telling me about Juarez bars that on
payday fill up exclusively with young working-class women, added
that he was shocked recently when a mob of young ladies who make
Johnson & Johnson surgical gloves for $40 a week climbed on a city
bus after the second shift and raucously proceeded to goose him.
Somehow that story reflects border women's new roles here. Those
who stay are playing an increasingly vital part in politics, from
running for office in El Paso to organizing leftist urban squatter
movements in Juarez, to exhorting rallies of the rightist National
Action Party. Those who leave and go farther north do it more and
more without men. And even when they remain and try to play the
same old roles — as maids, society ladies, housewives, mothers and
employees, for instance — things get skewed and twisted by
draconian new demands on everybody. The resulting fray produces

much tragedy: drug abuse, child neglect, bad health, spiritual malaise, hard feelings, corrosive rage. But there's a hopeful side to these displacements. As advanced capitalism tries to make hay of their long-touted passivity and agreeableness, women and foreigners of both sexes "goose" it. They quit their jobs without giving notice, or they skip work every Monday and celebrate *San Lunes* Day. They organize, unionize, stage wildcat strikes. They march in demonstrations and seize a plot of land. They help each other find birth control, childcare, and abortions if need be. They risk harsh words, an arrest, a bop on the head.

The reasons these people give for their rowdiness may not fit the language we're used to. Our common ways of describing how a Third World woman decides to have three kids and no more, for example, may make us feel good about her "prudence" and the government's new birth control campaign. But they won't tell us much about how our exported IUDs, sterilization campaigns and arbitrary cultural assumptions have made this woman's neighbor feel guilty and unpatriotic about bearing a beloved and very much wanted fourth child. Nor can the language of our culture's interior verbalize what a poor Juarez woman tells herself: that she's become a leftist militant to trick both God and country, and get the fourth child that both have told her she must not have.

By looking and listening to the new people of the U.S., beginning with those who perhaps haven't yet crossed the line, we may feel some vertigo. But a little tipsiness might incline us to ask what's going on with all these immigrants. Where are they coming from? What vision do they offer us about a new economic and cultural order? And how do *we* fit in, without succumbing to fears that have already created "aliens" and "witches": today's new versions of "cooties, niggers, desegregation, miscegenatation, Reds and spies?"

Being on the U.S.-Mexico line has made me think constantly about such things. I hope these pieces will inspire additional thoughts and questions from others attracted to the border — whether in body or in spirit.

Many people lent ideas and inspiration to this book. I'm especially indebted to everyone, both locally and across both countries, whom I've worked with on immigration civil rights issues. Mexico City artist/activist Manny Anzaldo is one of them. Manny moved to Juarez a few years ago because he sensed the same excitement about going to the border from the south as I did when I came from the north. While he was here, he was constantly crossing — in both directions and through various means — all kinds of people, books, poems and translations, as well as buckets of paint. The murals that cover the concrete riverbank between El Paso and Juarez are his leavings, and each time he comes back for a visit people from both sides get together and slosh words and pictures on the international line.

Willie Delgadillo is another *fronterizo*: born in L.A., raised in Juarez, equally at home and equally estranged in both countries, and a pleasure to explore either with. A group of El Paso midwives, including Diane Holzer, have impressed me with their passion for living and working on the border. Lupe Borjon, a street vendor, has shared with me her family's troubles and hopes, as well as the inspiration of her quiet dauntlessness.

Thanks also to editors and publishers. Ellen Willis, formerly my editor at the *Village Voice*, treats writers with utmost respect. That, and her interest in exploring the edges of already controversial issues, have helped my past journalism. Marty Gottlieb, ex-editor-in-chief at the *Voice*, also encouraged my work on sex abuse hysteria at a time when probably no other major publication would have touched it. Bobby and Lee Merrill Byrd offered hospitality and friendship as we put these pieces together.

Finally, I want to thank former New Jersey daycare teacher Kelly Michaels, who was unjustly accused five years ago of horrible crimes against children. Despite her false conviction and imprisonment, Kelly has maintained her innocence, her sanity, and a generous curiosity about the world around her that is breathtakingly gutsy in light of the horrors she's suffered. I'd hoped this book could close with some of her writing about life beyond yet another border — i.e., one bounded by the bars of a women's prison. But the threat that publication might jeopardize Kelly's safety proved insurmountable and finally forced us to pull her work. Even so, her spirit remains in these pages as we wait for the time she'll be free to write her own book.

The Eyes of Texas Are Upon You

 Reyna would probably look poor no matter what she wore. She's got what she calls a beggar's body, meaning any hand-me-down you give her will fit, whether you're five feet or five foot nine. Her legs are too big and too soft, her chest too small. A couple of years ago, when she was 23, her stomach started hanging after her second spontaneous abortion in two years, following one or two of the illegal kind — the kind that in Mexico they call "provoked." For birth control now, Reyna sometimes shoots herself up with a Depo-Provera-like hormone that makes her periods last two weeks. She stops them with injections of ergot that she buys over the counter at the corner *farmacia* along with a hypodermic syringe.

Reyna's body is typical of the working-class Mexican woman, but her complexion is something else. When she walks down the street, men yell "Güera!" — the same thing they call the blond gringas from Wisconsin who are down on the border for the weekend looking to get bombed or for a bargain on Don Quixote statues.

If you could isolate a patch of her skin, or maybe the iris of an eye, you'd almost swear she was anglo. She's got this pink look about her, a blue-eyed look, even though her eyes are really brown. Even with a trace of Aztec in her cheekbones, Reyna's coloring would be worth American dollars if she could just figure out how to dress it up in the proper makeup and wardrobe.

But Reyna's taste in fashion is pure Ciudad Juarez, which is where she lives. Juarez, on the south side of the U.S.-Mexican border about 30 feet from El Paso, has over a million people, twice as many as 15 years ago. There's a little part of downtown, the part where the houses have colonial Spanish wrought iron, that proves Juarez used to have a textbook history. But now it's more the medical kind, history written in cardboard shacks, social pathology out of control.

It's fitting then that Reyna, who came to Juarez from a little town in downstate Chihuahua like all the other people who can't make a living in the countryside anymore, should have a swollen, teeming look. She favors wobbly high-heeled sandals with tight plastic straps, shiny royal purple dresses with patent leather belts, magenta fingernail polish, peacock blue mascara, lumpy fire-engine lipstick. It's a look geared to the budget and the yearning of someone who lives in a crumbling, $15-a-month room with no toilet, but revs up the blow-drier every morning before stumbling bleary-eyed to the seven to three shift at the multinational plant. Someone who hunches over printed circuit boards or industrial sewing machines all day, earning 40 cents an hour doing what some American worker in the Rust Belt used to do for ten times that much.

The 40 cents wasn't putting much meat on the two kids' bones, so Reyna decided to go to Albuquerque, 250 miles north. Her husband, Roberto, had just found a $4-an-hour TV repair job by sneaking past the U.S. Border Patrol checkpoint on Interstate 25 near Truth or Consequences, smuggled in the back of a semi. Reyna didn't have the money to pay another smuggler, so she begged and borrowed enough for an off-peak airline ticket to Albuquerque. She decided she'd take her chances at the El Paso International Airport.

But first, she contacted her fashion consultant, Lupita. A college-educated Trotskyist from Mexico City, Lupita was up on the border organizing for one of the Fourth Internationals. She wore Italian leather sandals that looked nicer instead of crummier the older they got, wire-rimmed glasses, and Wranglers. Unlike Reyna, Lupita was thin — but in a healthy way, the way that in Mexico they call *proteinizada*. Literally, that means you can afford to eat milk, cheese, fish, and meat regularly, maybe even for snacks. Figuratively, it means you've got the whole gestalt, the Look, that would make you blend into any major airport in the world.

Lupita had El Paso's version of the Look, and then some. She could breeze right past U.S. Customs at the international bridge without the agent even batting an eyelash as he asked

"Citizenship?" She ought to be featured in Women's Wear Daily.

Reyna and lots of other people around here would agree that Lupita makes an exciting fashion statement, though it has nothing to do with the turquoise and handwoven Native Americana that come to mind when most people think of Southwestern stylishness. This isn't Santa Fe we're talking about — it's El Paso, the poorest large city in the U.S. There are half a million people here and a quarter of them are eating courtesy of food stamps and emergency pantries. Several thousand living a few blocks from the luxury Westin hotel downtown bathe at gas stations and share outdoor toilets. They aren't street people, but upstanding churchgoers with steady jobs and apartments — even if they are tenements without indoor plumbing.

It's hard to imagine fashion trendiness in a city so impoverished that clothing is sold by the pound, where fortunes have been made in ready-to-wear by wooing clientele from the Salvation Army. Nevertheless, El Paso has its own Look, and Lupita found that trying to hip Reyna to its subtleties was even harder than explaining the theory of permanent revolution. "Get yourself some jeans and jogging shoes. And don't use eyeshadow," advised the Trotskyist. "I mean, a little's okay. But not too much. Also your fingernail polish. I don't know... it's a giveaway."

Reyna nodded her head and went shopping. Then she packed a bag and walked a couple of blocks from her apartment to the Rio Grande. A dehydrated stream trickling through two concrete embankments and many beer bottle shards, the river had even less water in it than usual. Had she crossed on foot, Reyna would barely have splashed her calves. But she wasn't taking any chances today on getting wet. She paid a dollar to a *burro* — a guy who carries people on his shoulders to the U.S. He dropped her off at the "Tortilla Curtain," a massive chain link barrier erected during the Carter administration to keep Reyna and the rest of her compatriots from invading Amer-ica. She picked out a roomy hole in the raggedy fence, hopped through, and invaded. America in this case was a south El Paso block filled with Korean-owned stores that hawk talking key chains, 99-cent digital clock dinner rings, and second-hand wardrobes baled like hay.

Reyna made it to the airport all right, but anyone could see she was one big faux pas. Purple jeans. Pumpkin colored jogging shoes. A peach polyester blouse with fluttery sleeves and a scalloped Emmett

Kelly collar with a big dip in the back where her horizontal bra strap stuck out like a T-square. A border patrol agent tapped her on the shoulder just as she reached the escalator. "Your citizenship," he said.

A few hours later Reyna had signed her voluntary deportation forms and was back in the Third World. Back to the two malnourished daughters, the toilet in the courtyard that you flush with a bucket, Lupita talking about how in Cuba there's a law that all kids must drink milk every day, the rickety tin closet filled with plastic high heels and crepe-papery skirts.

Next day she poked through the dust and beggars downtown and joined hundreds of other applicants roaming around the flat, manicured industrial parks on the outskirts of Juarez. She filled out forms at AMPEX (headquarters, Redwood City, California); RCA Components (headquarters, Indianapolis); Convertors de Mexico (American Hospital Supply, Evanston); FAVESA (Ford Motor Company, Detroit). Should she spend all day winding tape cassettes? Assembling TV components? Sewing disposable surgical gloves? Wiring automotive harnesses?

To tell the truth, these tasks appeal neither to Reyna nor to many of the other 86,000 workers in Juarez's mostly U.S. corporation-owned "twin plants." That phrase is just one more entry in late capitalism's newspeak lexicon, since El Paso's "twin" is usually a small office peopled with a mere handful of American citizen paper-pushers, while south of the river, the real plant is filled with hundreds or thousands of Mexicans — mostly women — fastening together all manner of loose gizmos exported from the high wage U.S. Once these products are assembled, they're shipped back to El Paso and points north, with duty paid only on the value added by the labors of people like Reyna.

On a nice day it seems all 86,000 of them are wandering from one plant to another changing jobs, while the personnel managers worry about the 10 percent a month turnover and mutter about moving the plants farther south where there's plenty of fresh, unjaded labor and the minimum wage is even less. Meanwhile, each plant has its own perks to inspire Reyna's loyalty. This one's got a good volleyball team. That one, a subsidized cafeteria and an annual beauty contest. The one over there just built a dressing room with showers.

Who cares? One's the same as another, Reyna figures. They all pay $3.30 a day plus a few bucks more at the end of the week if you've had perfect attendance. Which is hard to manage what with the hour's commute each way in the crammed, rickety public vans, the compulsory overtime, and the breakneck assembly line pace that usually drives Reyna to tranquilizers — she gets them over the counter, too — after a few weeks on the job.

Well, she would do it for awhile until Roberto sent his first paycheck from Albuquerque. Maybe she'd blown it, but *ojalá!* knock on wood! — he's figured out the Look.

What, exactly, is it? The Look has little to do with tacky textiles and poor fit, even though it's true that the glare of the desert sun is pitiless with people's lumps, rendering both polyester and pastel cottons useless camouflage. But that's not the point. Neither are entertaining sociological observations about how El Paso's poor look Goodwill; its lower-middle class buys lots of shiny stuff from the Koreans; the middle-middles, like public school teachers, wear lots of cautious, loose-fitting slubby knits that scream "Cotton! I can afford cotton!" (with the chicanas still wearing theirs in brighter colors than the anglos); and the really ritzy Hispanic society ladies are indistinguishable from their friends in Hadassah.

El Paso is still small enough so that you can see all these types walking down the same downtown street at noon. There are even a few residential blocks where anglo lawyers and chicano garment operatives live side by side. The historical restoration buffs in these old neighborhoods are vocally proud of the peaceful ethnic, if not class, mix — what they're quieter about is the embarrassing proximity of the Rio Grande.

In the Sunset Heights area, for instance, the city's turn-of-the-century ruling classes used to watch the Mexican revolutionary armies skirmishing just down the hill. But today, intimate little fajitas cookouts are awkwardly framed against a backdrop of miles of cardboard and adobe shacks lying across the river just a few blocks away. It's not uncommon at such parties for the hostess to answer a knock at the door and find an unequivocally polite young man asking in Spanish if she needs her yard done, as he stares, unequivocally starving, at the barbecue grill. The only unknown about such encounters is whether the young man is legal or illegal. How can you tell?

That question defines the nitty-gritty basics of the Look. Indeed, the true clothes horses of the border are *mojados* — the people who wet their own toes if they're horribly poor, or other people's if they're just terribly so, to cross the Rio Grande. They know that to keep your $40-a-week job without being deported, to escape to Chicago and get paid almost like a real American human, they must learn that certain weaves of sombreros practically scream "alien." Better to wear a baseball cap. But be sure the decal on it is a credible trucker motif. What about those boots? Are the edges of the heels cut exactly perpendicular to the ground, like they make them in Texas? Because if they're sliced on a slant, the wearer is from Chihuahua (or worse, even farther south). And how about that shiny black shirt with the purple zigzags? Take it off! Here, here's a T-shirt that says UCLA. Much better. That's the Look.

Not very exciting, you say? But you're not the judge. The final arbiter of fashion here is the border patrol, some 520 men and women in uniform who cruise about the El Paso area in bile green squad cars and Ram Charger vans with bars on the windows, checking out everyone on the streets, determining who has the good taste to be allowed to live and work here in peace, and who shall be spun through the endlessly revolving door of deportation, illegal reentry, deportation that keeps workers trapped in the sub-minimum wage and sub-minimum life sector of the U.S. economy.

The ritual used to be a lot easier on everyone. Until 1848, when the U.S. took most of what's currently the Southwest away from Mexico, there was no border here at all. And until 1903, there wasn't even a federal agency to screen or regulate immigrants coming into the U.S. When the border patrol, our only national police force, was first funded in 1924, there were only 75 agents to guard the whole 2000-mile southern border. A bunch of overwhelmingly anglo good ole boys who liked to think of themselves as Texas Rangers, they wore Smokey the Bear hats, rode horses, and took great pride in tramping through the desert for days, injun-style, following the tracks of lonesome smugglers. As far as wetback cotton pickers were concerned, they could pretty much hop over the border anywhere and anyhow they felt like.

Things aren't so casual anymore though, especially since immigrants have lately expanded their geographic and economic horizons far beyond stoop labor. And since the mid-1960s, U.S. corporate investment has gotten pretty migratory, too, bidding adiós to the falling rate of profit in the sleepy, inflation-ridden world of capital-intensive industry like steel or autos. The Promised Land now lies over the border and across the seas. Or else it's pizza huts, nursing homes, any-thing that's young, union-free, low-skilled, labor-intensive, and mini-mum-wage. Not so good for uppity citizens watching their old, well-paid jobs turn into labor history artifacts. But perfect for wetbacks who know their place.

Illegal aliens have always made great scapegoats during hard times and great people to ignore during good times. It used to be you could gauge the health of the economy by the Immigration and Naturalization Service's arrest statistics: post-Korean War recession of 1954, 1.1 million wets busted. World War II prosperity of 1943, only 16,000. Agricultural-industrial boom of the 1920s, about 4,000 a year. Yet shortly afterward, in the first years of the Depression, hundreds of thousands of Mexicans were encouraged to leave the U.S. "voluntari-ly" by welfare officials who threatened them with deportation and by railroads who kindly paid their way to Mexico. Ofelia Tapia, an El Pasoan who was in kindergarten then, remembers how the border pa-trol paid a $5 bounty to people who reported illegals like her mother.

"The neighbors would turn her in. Sometimes the migra" — the INS — "would put her in jail. Sometimes they'd send her back to Juarez. I was an American citizen but I'd have to go, too. We'd just wade across the river again after awhile."

What's novel about the most recent wave of mojados is that for the first time in U.S. history, large numbers of Mexicans and other Third-Worlders are coming here not during boom times, but in the midst of economic stagnation. That should come as no surprise, though, since postcapitalism's very efforts to jack up its falling profit rates have naturally fueled the global wanderings of people as well as money.

With immigration reform in the air, it's popular in border circles to do the usual cyclical bitching about how the invading brown hordes are bankrupting the county hospitals and taking everybody's jobs. But most people who've been here awhile know the border is one big bantustan dotted with a comfortable supply of Baskin-Robbinses and K-Marts. After all, if God hadn't wanted us to have $1.50-an-hour maids, waitresses, and minimum-wage mechanics and onion pickers, He wouldn't have created the border patrol. Chase them around in a squad car, kick 'em back to Juarez every once in awhile, and they'll work hard without demanding things like social security benefits or public health care.

But the good Lord only allocated a certain number of migras in the federal budget, and you won't find too many of them in Kansas City, Chicago, or Boston. That's why Reyna had her problems at the airport: "We're concentrating our manpower on apprehending people bound for the U.S. interior," an INS spokesperson said recently.

That effort has enveloped El Paso in a quiet state of siege the past few years. The Border Patrol's got the Rio Grande planted with a dozen closed-circuit TV cameras that transmit to a central control room run by an agent who knows exactly who's at the river at all times. Infrared body sensors and magnetic foot-fall detectors left over from the McNamara Line of the DMZ and from Cambodia and Laos are buried in the sandhills just outside the city. And the patrol's helicopters mutter over the historic neighborhood rooftops at dawn, lending an apocalyptic cast to the early morning dreams of local yuppies. Then there are the checkpoints on every highway leading away from the border; and the plainclothesmen working the Trailways station, Greyhound, Amtrak, and the airport. For good measure, they've been parking lately near midwifery clinics where Juarez women come to give their babies the ultimate silver spoon: birth in El Paso and automatic U.S. citizenship.

Under this barrage of technology and manpower even the impossibly blond, the securely anglo, get a bit shell shocked. Midwife Cindi Cushing, for instance, flew home to the East Coast recently after spending a year in south El Paso: "My mother and I were just walking out of the airport in Connecticut when a state trooper passed by in a green van. Without even thinking, I clutched my mother. I didn't even know I'd done it until she asked me what was wrong. Leaving El Paso too quickly is what it must have been like to go on rest and recreation to Honolulu too fast from Vietnam."

Then there are the people the El Paso border patrol actually gets its hands on: last year, for instance, the agency made 256,000 arrests. That's more than a quarter of the 1.3 million made in the entire country in fiscal year 1985. The only other district that arrested more mojados than El Paso was the one that covers the Tijuana-San Diego area. If you want to arrest 256,000 people, you have to stop a lot of folks, and there are only about 600,000 living in the entire region covered by the El Paso district patrol. About a tenth are mojados who've been here for years, perhaps married legal residents, had Texan kids, and bought homes. There are also 275,000 Mexican-

Americans, most of them not all that easy to tell from the illegals. There's a lot of leeway for mistakes. They happen.

Border patrol agents are only supposed to stop you on the street if they can put into words why they think you act or look illegal — the color of your skin, your accent, even speaking Spanish aren't supposed to count. But their decisions about who's got the Look of acceptable citizenship can be pretty arbitrary. I know some superproteinizado grad students and university professor types who've been stopped in their neighborhoods and asked, "¿De dónde eres?" A Chicano obgyn with a house in the ritzier part of town was watering his lawn once and they thought he was the yardboy.

If the protein people can't always master the Look to the migra's satisfaction, who can? The dilemma creates subtle self-doubt and image anxiety in mojados and citizens alike. After all, in the rest of America a person can do something legal or illegal, but on the border, being legal or illegal is a fact of daily existence. The INS and border patrol refer to this weird condition as your "status." It's even more bizarre to conceptualize dressing legally, and in El Paso, thanks to military and corporate chain department store aesthetics combined with limited disposable income, most people look like they take their fashion cues from the Cheryl Tiegs Collection at Sears.

That's what happens when a whole community is trying to maintain its dignity, not to mention its livelihood. To look American on the border: it's a style dictated by an agency that is now having internal discussions about calling down the armed forces to help secure the southern fringe, that blithers about Arab terrorists poised to swim across the river. It's a look full of paranoia, but certainly devoid of fantasy or irony. Not to mention pleasure.

It's puritanical, as described by Marta, an illegal live-in maid: "When you're crossing the river, don't wear bright colors. You don't want to stand out from other people. When in the United States, don't wear anything sexy or flashy. Stick to shorts or jogging pants. A knit shirt or a T-shirt. Tennis shoes."

It's boring: "Do what my illegal students from Juarez do," advises Ricardo Aguilar, a professor at the University of Texas at El Paso. "Just look like a yuppie."

It's obsessive, like Reyna's endless questions to me now: "You should wear cotton, right? And what about my heels? Americans don't wear them this high, do they? How about mascara? Eyeshadow?

I notice gringas do wear eye makeup. But it's not as bright as this shade, is it? Or is it?"

Border Patrolwoman Estella Henderson recently verified the basic rules. She is chicana and grew up in south Texas a few miles from the river. The surname came from marrying a fellow agent she met at border patrol training school in Georgia. Henderson is 29, dark, very slender and beautifully correct in her dark green military pants, shirt and cap, spiffy black leather boots, and belted revolver. She pays out of her own pocket to have the uniforms dry cleaned. She is a woman who cares about Looks.

She took me riding in her green van, down the dirt road by the Rio Grande, just after the sun came up. Out-of-towners are always shocked when they see what separates the United States from Mexico at El Paso: nothing worth mentioning. No fence for many stretches, no desert — just a slip of a river and its concrete beaches. In some parts you can almost hop across, or pay some guy a nickel and walk to America on his old two-by-four. At this time of morning, men are standing in the murky water in their underwear. Women are dismounting from the shoulders of the burros who've helped them avoid the ultimate El Paso fashion no-no: walking around in wet clothes.

The first shift is about to start in the factories, restaurants, golf courses, lawns and laundry rooms of the First World. The mojados wish Henderson would leave so they can get to work. They look expectant, despairing, wired for the chase. "In about 15 minutes they'll all of a sudden stampede together and we'll only be able to pick up a few of them and the rest will just run between those tenements and disappear into the shopper traffic on South El Paso Street," says Henderson. She's been working since midnight. Soon she'll be off, and another shift of agents will spend the day cruising down the streets, staring, checking, stopping, deciding who does and who doesn't have the Look.

Back at the border patrol's downtown offices she gives me a few tips, indicating the group of 60 bleary-eyed men shuffling around in the peeling, graffiti-smeared holding pen. They're mostly the night's catch from the freight trains bound from El Paso to Kansas City, L.A., and Chicago. "See him?" Henderson points. "His hair is longer than they wear it around here. And that one over there. He's darker than people around here. And see that goatee? He's not from El Paso because men hardly wear beards here."

"Dangerous business, riding freights," comments a Puerto Rican patrolman. "They see us coming and try to run away. They get hurt. Two months ago a guy had his ankles cut off while he was running from us. And remember that lady last year who was hiding between the trains near the Border Highway and was changing her baby's diaper? Threw the baby to her husband just in time. Then she got sliced in two...."

There are other occupational hazards involved in getting to work in the morning if you're a mojado. Like the culvert the border patrol calls the Ho Chi Minh Trail. It starts right by the river, a few yards away from an El Paso café where they serve great chile rellenos and superb frozen margaritas. After dinner and drinks you can stroll to the trail and chat with as many mojados as you want. They enter the culvert, which can be very muddy, and emerge a quarter mile away near the business administration building of the University of Texas. I met an old man there once with a bag of hedge clippers dangling from a plaster cast on his arm.

"I slipped while they were chasing me," he said. "Do you need your lawn done?"

Others try their luck running across Interstate 10, which runs to Houston and L.A. No time to look for traffic if the migra's on your heels.... The newspapers are filled with two-inch boiler plate about "Mexican nationals" run over gravely or fatally.

Then there are the drownings. The mojados see the migra coming and start running. They slip, and the current is fast. Or they're making their daily wade to America and suddenly hit a deep spot that wasn't there yesterday. That's what happened last summer to El Paso Times reporter Berta Rodriguez's uncle from Juarez. "He needed to come to El Paso to do some roofing work and it made him real nervous to cross illegally. He drank a lot of beer to get his courage up, so he was probably a little drunk. He went down in the river and never came up," Rodriguez remembers.

And there were the four women found drowned, raped, and strangled at the river this spring. One's still unidentified; one was 13 years old. They were all maids coming over to look for work. The man who confessed said he got them by offering to help them cross without getting wet. "Too bad about those girls. They must have been naive," says Marta, the maid who knows not to look sexy on this side.

"Yeah, I worked in a twin plant once," she says, wrinkling her nose. She much prefers being in El Paso and working for people like her former employer Carol, a divorced mother of two preschoolers who, after five years as a medical transcriber at a major hospital, was earning $5 an hour. The kids had terribly British names, blond hair, were bilingual thanks to Marta, and refused to speak a word of Spanish outside the house. Day care for Heather and Stephanie was out of the question, since it costs $80 a week for two kids — hardly affordable on Carol's typical El Paso salary. Marta, on the other hand, gladly slept on Carol's couch, tended the children, and even kept the house for only $40 a week. While Marta served the nachos and tamales at suppertime, Carol would sit around wondering if she was eligible for foodstamps. When her friends came to visit, they would light up a joint and say, "Have the maid bring us something cold."

Marta likes to swagger and snicker when she talks about the migra. "Once I was crossing over with four girlfriends and this migra saw us and I said, `Run, girls!' and we ran and ran with him right behind. I was the ringleader, and I made us run forever. But then I looked back and he had his gun pointed at us. I told my amigas to freeze. He huffed and puffed all the way back to the pen. `Oh girls!' he kept saying," Marta laughs.

But sometimes she gets wistful. "I tried to bring my little girl over — she was two years old then and still drinking out of a bottle. But she slowed me down so much that naturally I got caught at the river. They bused us all the way down to Ysleta (12 miles from downtown El Paso) and let us off on the Mexican side. There I was without a peso and had to wait a long time to hitch a ride back to Juarez. My little girl's bottle was empty...she was really sweating...a lady gave me money for a lemonade. I called my mom and she took the bus from our house that night, a four-hour trip to Juarez. `I'm taking the baby back with me,' she said. And naturally as soon as she left I crossed the river with no trouble.

"How often do I see my little girl? Well, every couple of months. At least the last few months she's gotten old enough to remember I'm her mother.

"The scariest experience I ever had with the migra was one day when I had to take Heather" — Carol's daughter — "down the street to kindergarten and Stephanie (the two-year-old) was still asleep. So I left Stephanie in the crib and locked her in the house. On the way back from walking Heather to school this migra drove past me and stopped. *¡Gracias a dios!* I had on my jogging shorts and a sweatshirt and my hair was a mess. I started trotting and the migra said in English: 'Good morning. Out for a run?' 'Oh yes,' I said in English, and he said, 'Have a good day!' and drove off. Pretty good, huh? But, *dios mío*, imagine if he'd caught me and kept me for hours and deported me to Juarez, with the baby locked up in that apartment? Every time I think about it I still shake," she says.

I had told Marta I would be riding with an Hispanic border patrolwoman. "If it's the skinny one, she's the one who's picked me up twice. Ask her please, why does she do this to her own people?" Marta said.

"Oh, they ask me that all the time," Henderson answered. "If it's a man who asks, I say, 'It's your job to build rock walls.' If it's a woman I say 'It's your job to take care of other people's children. And it's my job to catch you.'"

Earlier this summer Henderson's patrolman husband, Carl Ray (a.k.a. Bear), was driving his van full of wets through south El Paso when a young Hispanic beckoned him over, ostensibly to point out more illegals. Bear asked the man for his papers. Instead he received two thumbs in his eyes, several bites, and knife slashes in the arms. His assailant, strangely enough, was a U.S. citizen. The Hendersons and their supervisors blamed the incident on the fact that the perpetrator was high on something and "possibly a gang member." But Estella Henderson admits that "there's a lot of animosity...citizens will often try to interfere when you're questioning an illegal alien." As for the illegals themselves, though, "They don't get mad at me. They understand that I'm just enforcing the laws."

What does she think of the laws? "I don't know. I just enforce them," she says, steering past the Ho Chi Minh Trail.

"A lot of migras are pretty nice," says Marta, and her assessment is echoed by another maid, Vicki: "This gringo migra caught me but he was very helpful. He said American girls always carry purses with them and if I get myself one, he won't pick me up the next time. But the Mexican" — i.e. Hispanic — "migras are the meanest," Vicki says.

Cesar Caballero, a chicano and an activist in El Concilio de El Paso, an umbrella group of Mexican-American organizations, agrees. "A lot of us in the late '60s and early '70s pushed for Hispanic representation in all jobs, including in the border patrol," says Caballero.

"In the barrio when I was a kid we used to play migra instead of cow-boys and Indians. The border patrol would be the bad guys and the il-legal aliens were the heroes. The object of the game was to run fast and find real good places to hide. Now chicanos are the biggest *cabrones* — the biggest bastards — in the migra."

"Maybe they join the border patrol to show they're really part of the establishment," says Professor Aguilar. "They've been raised in fear of the migra and it's their way of proving to themselves that they're not afraid."

"Sometimes I think we've created a monster," Caballero says.

As for Henderson, though she grew up on the border, she doesn't recall having any relatives on the Mexico side. She does remember being stopped many times by the Border Patrol and being asked about her citizenship.

"I never minded that. I figured they must have a good reason," she says. "They were doing their job. I'm doing mine." And it's a good job — a great job for someone who hasn't finished college in a region where a secretary averages $10,000 a year. Not counting the extra she makes in overtime and shift differentials, Henderson is making in the low 20's after only two years with the patrol. She wants to take some classes and finish up her bachelor's in law enforcement. And she and her husband are planning a baby soon.

She'll probably need her own maid then.

Meanwhile, what Henderson and her fellow agents say they en-joy most is plainclothes duty at the airport. The wets there have more money, more savvy, and more style than your average pedestrian house servant. "That's where you find the challenges: the ones with forged documents, even people who've been living here for years and maybe have their own businesses," Henderson says. "But you can still tell they're illegal. Like, they could even wear expensive jeans, but they're too brand new. Or they don't fit quite right. These people walk around looking uncomfortable and nervous. You develop a sense for who they are."

But not always. Lately the airport has gotten notorious as a place where chicanos say they've been questioned and even detained by overly hardworking migras. Caballero, a university librarian, says he gets stopped every time he tries to catch a flight. That he's now a reg-ular habitué of airports rather than the south El Paso slum where he spent his boyhood makes little difference. "It doesn't matter how far you've come in the world," he says. "They're going to hassle you if you're brown."

On the other hand, every time the Border Patrol stops somebody like Caballero, presumably some real wets are making it through the line somewhere else. Despite the state of siege, you can still get over, still master the Look. Especially if you have help from the kind of people who get L.L Bean catalogs in the mail.

Like one guy active in the sanctuary network who dresses Salvadoran and Guatemalan refugees for their trips farther into El Norte. "I lent this one man my pink Izod shirt, an old pair of Nikes, some jeans, and these yucky sunglasses. He got through," says the networker. "But you'd be surprised how many Central Americans absolutely refuse to dress up to go to the airport. We'll say `put on this alligator shirt' but they'll say `No. I want to dress like me. I am not an American.' Here they've made it to El Paso after escaping death squads, walking through Mexico, maybe being raped by the police there... and all they have to do is this one last thing to get up to Chicago or Canada. And they won't. What is it? Pride?"

Or maybe it's just too enervating to make the effort. Americans are supposed to have an instinct for ever-changing ready-to-wear in their blood. And Mexicans have been raised so close to this cynical sense of style that it's not much work for them to grasp the concept that wearing plastic shoes last year would have screamed "illegal," but now it's okay because all the best gringa girls have their Jellies. For people who've spent their lives hundreds of miles rather than hundreds of yards south of the Look, trying to learn it quickly may be too hard. Some may find it better to hang onto their un-self-conscious foreignness, saving that precious élan that can get you past some pretty tight spots. "You'd be surprised at the number of people who go to the airport in their own clothes and still get through," the sanctuary worker tells me. He says that one in three Central Americans makes it past the border. The Border Patrol says two in three Mexicans do. And if they get far enough away, they leave the Look behind them.

But what will happen from Los Angeles to New York and through the heartland, if enough citizens take seriously the immigration reform talk of once and for all getting rid of the wets, the illegals, the mojados? Will the Rio Grande upstage the coasts as a mecca for style? Will all the brown people in America have to draw a straight line between citizenship and Reeboks?

The mojados are in every city now, in just about every factory, every field, every take-out joint and sit-down restaurant everywhere in America. No matter what laws are passed against them, the economy will keep needing them. So we might as well ask whether we're also going to want the vans, the squad cars, the TV cameras, the guns, the migras, and yes, even the soldiers everywhere in America. That's what it would take, after all, to nationalize the tyranny of the Look.

Epilogue

Shortly after the above was written, Congress passed the 1986 Immigration Reform and Control Act, popularly known as "Simpson-Rodino" — or, to people like Reyna and Marta, "La Simpson."

La Simpson was touted by the government and mainstream media for its provision of "amnesty" to almost three million undocumented immigrants. In addition, the law requires every job applicant to show documents proving U.S. citizenship, residency or other valid immigration status. Any employer who knowingly hires a person without such papers is supposed to be fined or even criminally penalized. By thus destroying their chances of making a living, the new law promised to discourage the arrival of more mojados.

That has been La Simpson's shiny public relations side. Reality is much uglier, considering the fate of immigrants who arrived after the law's 1982 "amnesty" deadline. It's estimated that there are another three million of these people in the U.S., and, though INS arrest figures went down after the 1986 law took effect, they soon rose again and now are running to more than a million annually. Daily, more and more mojados continue to cross the border.

What's changed, though, are their working and living conditions. The biggest, best-paying companies, those that used to hire the undocumented, are generally toeing La Simpson's line and will no longer hire them — unless they show up at Personnel with expensive, phony birth certificates and forged social security cards. For those who can't afford this "tax," fewer job opportunities and further restrictions in social entitlements such as public housing mean destitution, even homelessness. Or, if they're lucky, the mojados still find grueling, subminimum-wage work in out-of-the-way places — maid jobs in private houses, for instance.

This may be why more and more undocumented newcomers are women. Until the mid-1980s, Third World natives who crossed the border were overwhelmingly men, who almost always left their families behind and sometimes never sent for them. But researchers are lately noting a dramatic rise in the percentage of women crossers. Often, they bring their children; almost always they support families. By hiding in traditional "female labor" locales — like in domiciles and mom-and-pop cafes that escape the eyes of La Simpson's enforcers — Third World women seem to be displacing U.S. minorities in the most oppressed sectors of the economy. Restrictive immigration laws assure that, whether they stay at home in their countries and labor in multinational plants or cross over to the First World, such women will almost inevitably end up at the bottom of the capitalist heap.

Meanwhile, on this side of the line, whether legal or mojado, Hispanics and other minorities continue to be inspected by the Eyes of Texas, eyes that keep looking farther north. A recent government study documented widespread employer refusal to hire people who "looked" or "sounded" like foreigners, even when they had a right to work. On the military front, the Border Patrol has augmented its staff by 50 percent since 1986; and within the last five years, the force has almost doubled. Not all the agents have stayed at the frontier. With the opening of patrol offices in cities like Albuquerque, Houston and Dallas, the border and everything it implies is extending into the U.S. interior.

And perhaps even more ominous than the prospect of a national police department combing the country for the darkskinned is that of the same body empowered to hunt down dope runners. As a ploy to get more funding and tougher laws, the Department of Justice and the INS since 1986 have collapsed drug trafficking and undocumented immigration into one big issue. In late 1990, Congress empowered INS officials, including Border Patrol agents, to use arms to make arrests not just for immigration offenses, but for any federal felony. Thus, one of the Patrol's main tasks now is drug interdiction — a situation that threatens not only the rights of immigrants and citizens, but their health as well.

To fight the "war on drugs," agents now routinely carry high-powered automatic weapons that can combine with poor training and racism to produce potent danger. My neighborhood lime vendor, for instance, a woman who crosses almost daily with her little girls in tow, described a recent scene near the "Ho Chi Minh Trail" in El Paso. It seems some unarmed but cheeky youths on the Mexican side of the river shot the "finger" at two Border Patrol agents. The officials responded by firing M-16 rifles into the air for several minutes, while the fruit vendor's nine-year-old daughter cried hysterically and screamed, "Mommy, they're going to kill us all!"

The incident ended without anybody getting hurt. Immigrants elsewhere haven't been so lucky. An American Friends Service Committee study done on the southern U.S. border between mid-1989 and 1990 found six deaths and eight serious injuries of Mexican nationals resulting from shootings by Border Patrol and other law enforcement officers. These did not even include assaults on immigrants by civilian vigilantes who've picked up on the spirit of the times: such as the group of San Diego teenagers who Fox TV's *The Reporters* filmed donning combat fatigues and using BB guns to chase down immigrant families. Other crimes and indignities abound: like in South Texas, where summary detention and deportation of Central Americans seeking asylum has been termed a systematic violation of human rights by Helsinki Watch.

In response to the crisis created by militarizing immigration control, advocacy groups are forming in border cities as well as in interior areas with large immigrant communities. Increasingly, activists and people of conscience are realizing that defending mojados and people who merely appear "foreign" is an urgent civil rights issue. As such, it affects all Americans, no matter what our ethnicity, our citizenship or residency status may be — and no matter how we act in the world through our speech, haircuts, lipstick shades, clothing, our bodily movements ...in short, no matter how we choose to Look.

For more information about immigration rights and how to get involved with groups working to protect them, contact the American Friends Service Committee's Immigration Law Enforcement Monitoring Project, 3635 W. Dallas Street, Houston, Texas 77019; telephone number 713-524-5428.

— 1986

America Don't Want No Angry Men

Margie is a paralegal for an agency that does amnesty work brought on by the new immigration reform law, which here in El Paso means work mostly on behalf of Mexicans. She does political asylum and refugee petitions, too, mostly for people from the more battered parts of Central America. Because Margie is government-approved, she's one of the few people besides attorneys allowed into the "Processing Center" — the Immigration and Naturalization Service's official name for the local illegal alien jail.

Even though I'm no Processing Center regular, my work with an immigrants' rights group has given me a taste of the place. We get calls — always collect, always desperate — from men who have been in for months with no lawyer or money for bond, men who say their clothes were taken by guards, men who say they've been beaten. There used to be this Cuban who would get on the pay phone and dial random numbers in El Paso and Juarez, and when someone answered in Spanish, he'd ask for shirts. The INS guards laughingly recall how he was constantly getting parcels in the mail and running a regular haberdashery behind bars. It seems a lot of people around here have a soft spot for the detainees, though hardly anyone knows just where they're kept since the center is hidden on the desiccated fringes of the city, behind the main Border Patrol office.

For years, most illegal aliens have called these places *corralones*. It comes from the same word as "corral" — a holding pen for animals. Before you get to the El Paso pen, you pass a huge lot filled with disabled Border Patrol Ram Chargers that broke down during street and desert chases. The vehicles are coated with dust, and on the windshields, fingers have rubbed the Spanish for "Fuck the INS." Lately, the agency has tried to spruce up its image, be more user friendly. So they've put up a new welcoming sign at the center. It says "Corralon."

Margie spends a lot of time there interviewing people who, when they got to the U.S., either turned themselves in to Customs at the airport or sneaked across the Rio Grande and got picked up because their clothes or their papers didn't look right. She herself is chicana, in her early forties. She keeps kiddie carseats in the trunk, tells you they're for the grandchildren when they visit, and you can't believe it because she looks too young. The *corralon* guards flirted with her the Saturday morning we walked down the drab halls past the employees' Coke machine. She had told the INS bureaucrats that she would be bringing in "emergency assistants," three sanctuary and immigration activists, to help process nine Africans who she had told me on the phone the night before wanted to emigrate to Toronto and "need to be done real quick." So the four of us headed for the interviewing room to meet the Somalis, who sat at a table in a long room bisected by plexiglass laced with chicken wire.

They were all young men in their twenties, lighter-skinned than I had expected — more Semitic than Hamitic, with long bodies and faces. Their hair was softer and looser than that of sub-Sahara Africans, and with the sun in the exercise yard glaring behind them, you could see right down to their scalps.

Except for what I had gleaned the night before from a garage-sale reference book, I knew nothing about these men or their country. The book said that in ancient times Somalia was called the Land of Punt, that most of its people are still grouped into nomadic, Muslim tribes, and that two principal exports are frankincense and myrrh.

Frankincense and myrrh. I tried to imagine these nine young men as Magi. Or sheiks, sultans. Shakespeare would have said Moors and cast them as Othellos. But not today. Now, instead of robes and turbans, they wore identical navy blue polyester windbreakers, courtesy of the *corralon*.

"Here's your guys," said McGuire, a chicano guard who sat at a little desk near the interview room. McGuire slumped over his cup of coffee and half closed his eyes — he was used to refugee interviews and didn't seem to notice that these were not your typical applicants.

We'd all talked to the regulars before — the Central Americans; we knew the blacks and whites and grays of their reasons for seeking political asylum. But Somalis? We had no idea why, but we got down to work anyway.

When you do an asylum or refugee application, you sit on one side of the chicken wire with your questions. On the other side is the detainee with his answers. You read your part off the form: When were you born? How many years of schooling did you have? Tell me every address you've lived the last ten years. Where, exactly, did you enter America? What terrible things happened to you back in your country? If you return, what awful things will *probably* happen? And what horrors will *surely* transpire?

Then the detainee gives you his reasons. There are many, some transparent, or at least translucent. There's the 17-year-old Guatemalan whose nuclear family has been decimated by Death Squads. He's ridden and stumbled for months through Mexico and has a facial tic that won't go away. There's another Guatemalan, a woman (released without bond because the *corralon* doesn't have room for females), whose army officer husband made her do S&M with him until she couldn't take the rubber and whips anymore, and besides, he's got connections to the CIA and uses things worse than rubber and whips on his prisoners, and she's ready to document that with Amnesty International.

But there are people with murkier reasons. Like the 25-year-old Salvadoran who's been here off and on since age 17, speaks Cheech and Chong English, was deported three times, the second time after being busted for shoplifting, the third time after he served time for dealing coke in California. The last time he was home, he says, the Death Squad mistook him for his guerrilla brother, imprisoned him for weeks, tortured him with wires, and sliced him with a machete. But when he tells you this, he talks so casually, displays his long, deep scars with such matter-of-fact absence of tics, that you wonder whether this guy's Death Squad was in El Salvador. Or was it really a street gang in L.A.?

But whatever his motives for leaving his country, whatever the ambiguities of his desire to come north, the asylum interview strains all the confusion and muddiness through *corralon* chicken wire. And by the time the reasons get to your side, they're sieved pure and true. Sign here, you tell the detainee. He does. You aim the camera, he poses. Now it is official: he is a seeker of political asylum or refuge. And you staple his picture to a set of forms.

So now here were these Somalis, and they were not Guatemalans or Salvadorans. They looked at us with an oddly open look, stared into our eyes gravely, their bodies and heads held straight. They held themselves and stared with the same look you see in National Geographic pictures of tribal warriors or peasant children, or in old daguerreotypes of citified adults in the Americas or Europe of a bygone century. They looked like they hadn't yet reached our epoch, our ease in slouching affably before minor officials and cameras.

As we rushed to fill in nine multi-paged forms, we learned only a little about them. They told us they were all from Somalia's capital, Mogadishu, which my book said has charming Italian architecture and streets teeming with camels. We learned that in this town over-run with camels, they had worked as auto mechanics in places with names like the Brothers Shop, as kitchenboys in the Zeno Restaurant, for a certain number of shillings that worked out to about $50 U.S. a month. One of them, who said his name was Muhammed, seemed to be the leader of the rest. He spoke good English — even saying "You know?" between utterances. I complimented him on his command of the language. He almost smiled. "Thanks," he said, "but it is because of the English colonization of our country. Imperialism." I looked at him. He glanced around, saw that McGuire had opened his eyes, and got confused. Then he looked grave again.

We got to the part about date of birth and they just kept shrugging. They seemed bewildered, or stoned on something they'd smuggled into the *corralon*. Muhammed finally explained that in Somalia, birthdays are neither celebrated nor attended to.

"What do we put down where it says date of birth?" we asked Margie.

"Just leave it. I'll write in something," she said.

Through all this McGuire sat, shifting his weight from one haunch to the other. A walkie-talkie on his little desk spat out garbles of pan-*corralon* vigilance: "Three more Cubans going in to be fed...Lopez number one-nine-four-four-three-eight-seven entering the yard...." McGuire fidgeted, as though trying to please some invisible supervisor skilled not only on the walkie-talkie but also in hiding behind corners and spying on underlings.

Margie was used to INS people, people like McGuire: "I really can't complain about those guys," she said later. With McGuire she smiled, flirted and said, "I can deal with the Guats. Or give me a Nic or a Sal. But the Cubans, forget it!"

"Just can't take those Cubes, huh?" McGuire said, and laughed. Sometimes he and Margie talked in Spanish and smiled and laughed even more.

She smiled at the Somalis, too, and was brusque only because there were so many of them, so many forms to process and this was her day off, and she wasn't getting paid. So at first she was short with them, but we soon realized that Somalis were easy. Not one had ever married, ever had children. In this they were unlike the young men of Central America, with their plethora of dependents conceived both in and out of wedlock. The Somalis' Muslim prudence, abstinence and bachelorhood, on the other hand, promised to redeem not only the population crisis, but our Saturday afternoon as well. With no extraneous addresses, wedding dates or birthplaces to worry about, we could leave pages and pages of the application forms blank. We'd be out of the *corralon* by lunch.

Now it was time for the heart of the matter: why do you need asylum? Muhammed spoke for the others. They'd all been arrested and put in jail in Magadishu, he said.

"Why is that?" we asked.

"Because we did anti-government activities, because see, we were in the SSDF."

"SSDF?" we said.

"Yeah, SSDF."

"What is that?"

"Somalia Salvation Democratic Front, you know."

"Oh. Somalia Salvation Democratic Front. OK. Uh-huh. All of you. Right?"

"Yeah, all of us. We are all friends. And we are afraid they hurt us or kill us if we go back to our country, and we got forged Tanzanian passports and flew to New York. And now we are here. We want to go to Toronto. We have aunts and uncles there. They have grocery stores, you know."

Muhammed gestured to the others, and on cue, each pulled out a paper with handwritten English. The texts, signed with names like Abdullah, Yusuf and Ahmad, all scrawled and halted in different ways. But always, they told the same story: Somalia Salvation Democratic Front. Canadian grocery stores.

"Have you guys ever heard of the SSDF?" I asked the other two sanctuary activists.

"It must have something to do with Ethiopia," one of them said.

If they heard us, the Somalis still didn't volunteer any information. As it was, we had no idea how to make small talk about salvation democratic fronts in countries with nomads and camels. Canadian grocery stores were almost as difficult, what with the plexiglass and concrete echoes that made conversation impossible. So we stapled papers together. Then we went to the exercise yard for pictures.

Margie was in high spirits as she loaded her Polaroid. *"Buenos días!"* she chirped to Muhammed. "That means Good Morning. That's Spanish!" The young man nodded and gazed at the camera, arranging his face into noble, stony-faced dignity.

Margie aimed the camera. "Smile!" she said.

He rearranged his face. It looked even more grave.

Margie frowned. He frowned too.

"No, No," Margie said. The flash indicator light had warmed up long ago. She was getting impatient.

She looked at McGuire. He shrugged and rose from his chair.

"Smile!" he commanded. "You want to get out of here, don't you? "

The young man nodded blankly.

"To immigrate?" McGuire said.

"Immigrate. Yeah," he said.

"Then look happy. Smile. Smile! America don't want no angry men!"

"Actually they're headed for Toronto," Margie said.

"Oh. Well, Canada don't want no angry men either," said McGuire. He laughed.

Muhammed pondered these words. Then he nodded, turned to his countrymen, and with a loud voice, issued orders in a flowing tongue. The men all lined up and Muhammed struck a pose. The others dutifully copied it. In the glare of the desert behind them, their skulls shone naked, delicate.

"Now you've got it!" said Margie.

"Move out of that sun," said McGuire. "Good. Cheese!"

And so were nine refugee applications completed, supported by photographs of nine men — men all with their eyes narrowed just so, shoulders slouched, palms rotated ever so slightly, their rows of teeth bared wide. Thus, with nine instamatic smiles, did the Somalia Salvation Democratic Front enter history. As for those of us who'd been there awhile, we stopped at the guards' vending machine, bought Diet Cokes, then drove back to our Saturday afternoons.

— *1987*

Maria del Refugio ("Cuca") Gonzalez Vasquez

 At about 3 o'clock on a hot Friday afternoon in June, 1985, Diana Duran received a call informing her that Michelle, her two-month old child, was in a hospital emergency room. The baby had just been brought in by two young girls, the caller said, and she wasn't breathing.

Diana is the wife of El Paso attorney Frank Duran, and when she answered the phone she was working at her husband's law office. She thought the call was a hoax. After all, she had phoned the house just a few minutes before and talked to the maid, who said the kids (there were three others besides Michelle) were all fine and that they were playing. Despite her skepticism, Diana rushed from the office in central El Paso and drove to the family's Lower Valley home. When she got there she found all the doors open, the stove on and the maid gone. The other children — six-year old Cristina, four-year-old Anita and one-year-old Frank, Jr. — were upstairs by themselves. Frank and Anita were in the bathroom, smeared with lipstick, and Cristina was yelling, "The maid took Michelle!" Diana packed them into the car and headed for the hospital.

There, she was led to the emergency room, where 10-week-old Michelle lay pierced with IV lines. A doctor again told Diana the

---

Note: The names of the defense and prosecuting attorneys, police and jurors mentioned in this story are authentic. All others have been changed.

baby wasn't breathing on her own. A few minutes later, she went into the waiting room and saw the maid, who was crying. Herself completely distraught, Diana asked what happened. The maid said she'd gone into the bedroom where Michelle was sleeping and found a small baby pillow over her face. Diana kept asking if the baby had fallen. The maid kept saying no. Why, then, Diana asked, hadn't she called the law office when she found Michelle not breathing? "I don't know your number or name," the maid answered.

Her ignorance about the details of her employer's life was feigned, but for her part, Diana definitely knew very little about the maid, who'd only been working for the Durans a few days. Her name, for instance, was Maria del Refugio Gonzales Vasquez; but Diana simply called her Cuca, which in Spanish is short for Refugio. She didn't know Cuca's age, either — she figured her to be somewhere between 18 and 20 — nor did she know exactly where she was from. Later, the authorities would ascertain that Cuca's hometown was Zaragoza, a small village in the southern Mexican state of Zacatecas. She had come up to the border to Juarez a few months before, following a migratory route well traveled by the men and women of her state. The men usually cross the Rio Grande illegally and press farther to jobs in places like San Antonio and Dallas. Women like Cuca, though, don't travel into the U.S. They stay on the border and work as domestics.

Actually, Diana was wrong about her maid's age — the day that Michelle Duran stopped breathing, Cuca was only 17. When she arrived in Juarez in the spring, 1985, she stayed with her cousins and her Aunt Paulina in a tiny cinder block and stucco house in the Galeana colonia on Calle Huajalpa, a dusty rut of a road without street signs, near the Channel 44 TV station towers on the hills that hem Juarez in on its southwest side. Cardboard shacks, goats and human waste snake up and down the local sierra and form the city boundary here. It's a place El Pasoans seldom venture to unless they are missionaries.

Cuca was the third of seven children. Back in her village, she completed only three years or so of elementary school; then, at age 13, she started caring for the house and the younger four siblings. That made her a good candidate for a maid's job, a mainstay occupation for poor, uneducated Latin American country women who migrate to towns. If Cuca had traveled no farther than the nearest big city, Zacatecas, she would have been hired as a live-in domestic or washer woman at $15 or $20 a week. Up on the border though, by 1985, servants' jobs were much better paid, since most young Juarez women were working in the twin plants for $25 or $30. The competition left uppercrust Mexican matrons no alternative but to offer at least that, or more, if they hoped to get and keep a good servant.

Right after she got to Juarez, Cuca was hired by a local family. She worked for them for two months, during which time her *patrona* never knew her last name either; nevertheless, as she later told a jury, she thought Cuca was a "very good girl." This *patrona* had a job herself, and her boss, when he had business in El Paso needing legal attention, dealt with Frank Duran.

The law offices of Francisco Duran, P.C., are on Montana Avenue, near the city art museum. Here, the beautiful old mansions of El Paso's turn-of-the-century ruling class have long since been converted to office space for attorneys wishing to avoid downtown's high rents, but who still want to stay close to the courthouses. Most of the Montana Avenue lawyers are Hispanics by birth. Frank Duran is more than that. He has, for example, gone to court for Trinity Coalition, a community group that lost its government funding to provide low-cost child care after a controversial Mexican-American nationalist took over the leadership. If not a militant, Frank Duran is at least active in legal issues related to Chicano politics.

While Cuca was working in Juarez, Diana Duran gave birth. She was 31, and this was her fourth child in six years. Now, in addition to the 6-year-old, there were three preschoolers, including two in diapers. The Durans were living in a multi-storied, Santa Fe style house, hand-built years ago by El Paso scion Winchester Cooley. It was a veritable hacienda, graced with a parade of arches on the veranda, a pergola in the backyard, fireplaces inside, and dark *vigas* sticking everywhere out of sparkling white stucco. It was the kind of home that, when new, had probably been kept up by two or three Mexican servants. But that custom had been dead for a few generations. Now there was a big family in the house, but when they decided to hire help, the Durans wanted only one maid. They asked their Juarez client to recommend someone. He in turn asked Cuca's *patrona*, and the deal was done. Cuca sneaked into El Paso illegally, and on May 28, a Tuesday, she began working at the Durans'.

With the move across the international boundary, her earnings probably approximated the typical El Paso live-in maid's salary: room and board plus $40 to $60 a week. In the U.S. interior this might seem scandalously low. But El Paso is a terribly poor city, where many legally resident women earn minimum wage, and $50 is about all they can afford for child care. For upper-middle-class families, though, the prevailing servants' wage is a fantastic windfall that supports mothers' days out, as well as much community volunteerism. But no matter who they work for in El Paso, Mexican maids seldom complain about their pay. After all, it's double the wage in the twin plants and mansions a few blocks south.

Other than the money though, conditions for maids are pretty similar on both sides of the border. Their workday typically begins at breakfast, and includes cooking, sweeping, mopping, vacuuming, making lunch, washing clothes, washing dishes, changing diapers, giving children baths, breaking up their squabbles, taking phone messages, dusting, sorting the laundry, ironing, breaking up more fights and cooking yet another meal. Work doesn't end until the supper dishes are put away. All this for people who aren't your own family, for children who are somebody else's. It's all the same, whether in El Paso or Juarez.

What makes El Paso different is the constant presence of Border Patrol vans. They trundle around neighborhoods and popular shopping areas, making work a prison for undocumented young women. Maids who venture outside their employers' homes constantly fear being picked up and deported; many therefore seldom venture out. In Cuca's case, even if she'd dared leave the house, the Durans lived in the Lower Valley, but her girlfriends, who were also maids, lived miles away on the East Side.

During the week there was little for her to do but work, and even as maids' jobs go, there was a lot to do. The house was enormous, and of course there were the four children. Cuca found herself taking care of everything at once. Diana would later recall scolding her about how "she would carry around Michelle when she would be doing housework. She would sort of just hold her around the waist with one arm and do work with the other hand." Cuca herself would later tell police that a few days after she started working for the Durans, "I was doing housework in one of the rooms downstairs...I had the baby in my left arm, I turned and the baby's head hit the wall. [S]he cried a little but she later quieted down [and] I didn't think it was of a serious nature."

Cuca managed the household on her own for long stretches of time, particularly while Diana was at the office working as her husband's administrative assistant. But weekends promised relief. On Friday, El Paso maids get their wages and the next two days off. On payday evening, while the middle-aged women return to Juarez to visit husbands and children, young, single girls dress up for a night on the town. Toting weekender bags, they perch in glossy flocks at the bus stops, or they board their *patronas'* cars and are chauffeured to friends' houses or to the international bridge. Friday night means dancing, maybe at the clubs on Alameda Avenue. Saturday night there's more partying, and with it a chance to meet a U.S. citizen man, maybe become his *novia*, maybe get married, maybe get legalized. Or if none of that happens, it's a time to meet young Mexican guys, meet friends and just have some fun. Sunday evenings, the migration reverses, and Monday a new week's drudgery begins.

Friday morning, June 7, was the end of Cuca's first full week on the job at the Durans', and she was looking forward to getting off work that Friday evening for the weekend. As usual, it was turning into a hot day. After breakfast, Diana took the older girls to the mall and dropped Frank Jr. off at her father's, leaving Cuca with baby Michelle. After lunch everyone returned home, but Diana almost immediately left for the office. An hour later, Cuca called her new *patrona*. One of her girlfriends was going to be spending that night alone in her employers' home. Cuca wanted to know if she could get off a little early to keep her company.

Diana said no. In fact, she told Cuca, she and Frank had a dinner engagement which preempted the maid's night off. Diana hung up. An hour later, Cuca called again. She wanted to make enchiladas for dinner but there were no corn tortillas in the house. Could the Señora bring some home? Diana was irritated. She told Cuca to prepare a different meal using the meat and potatoes in the fridge. Then she repeated that Cuca was not allowed time off that evening. And by the way, she asked, how were the children? Fine, Cuca said. Diana hung up again.

Fifteen minutes later, Michelle was unconscious.

At the hospital Cuca kept telling the story about the baby pillow. Diana didn't buy it, especially after another doctor told her Michelle had suffered a blow to the head. Cuca, meanwhile, had left the hospital, apparently after Diana fired her, and had returned sobbing to the Duran house, packed her things and disappeared. Diana spent all night at Michelle's side. On Saturday afternoon the infant was still not breathing on her own, and Diana went to her sister's home, where the other children were staying. While she was there, she later told authorities, the phone rang. It was Cuca's girlfriend, Alicia, demanding that Cuca be given her week's wages. A few minutes later, a man called and said that if Cuca wasn't paid, the Duran house would burn down. Cuca herself then called and began arguing with Diana about the money. "My child is dying!" Diana said, and hung up on Cuca. Shortly afterwards she returned to the hospital. Two hours later, doctors told her Michelle was in a coma.

In the predawn hours of Sunday morning, Diana dictated a lengthy statement to the police accusing Cuca of injuring Michelle and then trying to hide the truth about what happened. She also recalled heretofore forgotten details, such as that there were two empty Budweisers lying around on Thursday, and it wasn't Frank Duran who drank them. Cuca, meanwhile, left her girlfriend's house and returned to Aunt Paulina's in Juarez.

By Wednesday Michelle was still comatose, and the police wanted Cuca back in El Paso. They contacted her friend Cecilia and asked her to convince Cuca to return for a friendly chat. Cecilia went to Aunt Paulina's and brought Cuca back over the international bridge. It was the first time she'd crossed into the United States legally. Detective Alfonso Medrano was at the immigration office, waiting for her.

Back at the Crimes Against Persons office, Cuca told Medrano the story about the baby pillow and added that she had run with Michelle downstairs, put tap water on her chest and tried mouth-to-mouth resuscitation in a desperate attempt to revive her. She gave a two-page statement, which was typed out in English and translated orally by another Hispanic police officer. She signed her name, with the half-printed, muddy penmanship of the semi-literate. Medrano then arrested her and booked her into the county jail.

According to the young woman who shared her cell, Cuca spent the first days after her arrest poring over religious tracts. Then, on Saturday, she began weeping inconsolably. She asked for a detective, and late that night, she dictated a new statement. In it, she recounted the Friday afternoon call she made to Diana asking to be let off work early, and the frustration she felt when Diana refused to give her the night off. She remembered the second call, the one about the tortillas. She remembered feeling terribly angry, and in the midst of it all, the baby was lying in her bassinet on the kitchen table, crying and crying. Cuca remembered slapping Michelle and throwing her into the bassinet. But the infant still wouldn't stop crying. Cuca remembered putting her hand over the baby's mouth and nose then, and keeping it there. Finally everything was quiet. She remembered turning back to the stove, then hearing a gurgling in the bassinet. She remembered picking up Michelle. She was limp. Cuca tried to revive her, by shaking and shaking her.

Three days after the date of this second statement, Michelle died. Cuca was charged with reckless endangerment as well as with injury to a child — a first degree felony with a maximum sentence of life.

She was indigent and couldn't afford a lawyer. So as she sat in jail awaiting trial, the state assigned Cuca two young attorneys drawn at random from the public defender pool — Pablo Alvarado and Robert Anchondo. Anchondo remembers the case as one of the hardest he's ever taken. After all, not only was a child dead, but the father was a fellow attorney. "We felt for the Durans," Anchondo says. Nevertheless, his sympathy for Cuca went beyond professional obligation. "She seemed like a very sentimental, innocent girl," he recalls.

He and Alvarado decided that their best defense was two-pronged. First, they would argue that the two policemen's statements were meaningless because Cuca had no comprehension of her right to remain silent, and because she couldn't understand the English text of what she had signed. Second, Michelle's autopsy reports indicated that, whatever else happened to her, the only thing that made her die was brain trauma caused by being severely shaken.

And now, Cuca had a new story: that while in the bassinet, Michelle had gagged on a piece of food. Alvarado and Anchondo thus planned to argue that, while Cuca admitted shaking the baby, she'd done it not to hurt her, but in a panicked effort to save Michelle from choking.

During the weeks before the trial, the attorneys tried to make things as favorable as possible for their client. They moved to have her confessions quashed. They also requested that when the assistant D.A.'s referred to Cuca in front of the jury they "refrain from using such language as 'wetback' and 'illegal alien.'" The court denied the first motion and granted the second.

The state, meanwhile, planned to claim that Cuca deliberately hurt Michelle, and that, after putting the infant on her deathbed, she even demanded wages. But whatever the maid's motives had been, at the crux of the case there was inarguably a helpless baby — a dead one. The trial promised to be dramatic.

When it began, though, four months after Michelle Duran died, hardly anybody showed up. Cuca had no family in El Paso and the Durans deliberately stayed away. Even the pensioners who attend trials instead of dollar movies had chosen other entertainment — the divorce proceedings of State District Court Judge and Mrs. John McKellips. In the courtroom where Cuca was to be tried, attorneys went about the humdrum task of picking a jury (the defense was looking for people who themselves had children and maids). Meanwhile, over at the divorce trial, the parties were wrangling over $500,000 worth of community property and a two-story Spanish-style home; Judge McKellips was passing around photos of unkempt bathrooms to prove that his wife was a poor housekeeper, and Mrs. McKellips was accusing the judge of having sex with his campaign chairwoman and contracting genital herpes. For the media and the community, the pecadillos of the rich were much more glamorous — and, given local conditions, infinitely more escapist — than the common passions of a housemaid and her *patrona* on a hot Friday afternoon.

Ultimately, any drama in Cuca's four-day trial was of the abject kind. A jury of mostly Hispanic men and women, mostly blue collar and middle-income people, listened as Assistant D.A. Carole Pennock — petite, single, childless, and impeccably tailored — opened by reciting the details of Cuca's alleged wickedness: her calls to Diana Duran demanding money, the second confession and its talk of slapping, throwing, suffocating and shaking.

Amid all this sat the maid, now known officially as Maria del Refugio Gonzalez Vasquez, and never referred to as "wet" or "illegal." She was barely 18 now and, in her dark-colored, severely cut dress, she could have been a Red Cross girl out to collect donations for a Mexican charity hospital. But she was in court, in the United States, where she understood barely a word of English. A motherly looking woman, the court translator, sat nearby and buffered the State's accusations by converting them to Spanish.

Detective Medrano took the stand. He testified about the jailhouse confession, and Cuca's attorney cross-examined him in a lackluster attempt to show that his client had had no idea what she was signing (even though another officer had translated for her). Then, to explain why Cuca would deliberately have done the things she described in the confession, Diana Duran was sworn in. Stylish, agitated and weeping, she described what happened that afternoon in June, including the conflict between her and Cuca about the maid's night off. Cuca's friend Ceci also testified about the Friday night plans the two girls had made.

A doctor came on to tell the jury how dangerous it is to shake an infant, about how the resulting whiplash causes fatal destruction of the baby's brain and spinal chord. He also showed that, in order to cause such an injury, an adult would have to shake a baby very hard. In his expert opinion, the physician said, such force usually comes from a person who is extremely angry.

By the third day of the trial, the courtroom seemed cavernously empty. There were only two spectators besides myself. One was an elderly black man — apparently he'd tired of the McKellips divorce. The other was a dapper, Clark Gable-esque man who identified himself as an FBI agent and as Michelle Duran's uncle.

"I hate maids," he kept saying during a court recess. "They're ignorant and stupid!" He shook his head, partly in disgust, partly to dislodge a memory that would not go away. "You should have seen her," he said. He spread his hands at waist level. "She was about this big. Plump. And green eyes. Green eyes!" He turned then, and headed into the judge's office, as casually as if it were a public men's room. He didn't come back.

The jury, though, had to stick it out to the end — and it found itself in a quandary. On the one hand, according to panel foreman, Kenneth Jones, no one ever doubted Cuca had done something wrong. When she finally testified that Michelle gagged on a tortilla and that she shook her only to save the baby, the jury thought she was lying and believed that the confession was the more accurate version of what had happened.

The problem was, nobody wanted to punish Cuca. The jurors harbored more animosity towards the cops and the Durans than they did the maid.

"All of them were very hostile to the police testimony," Jones said recently. "It's not that they even cared whether or not [Cuca] was given her rights, or whether what she told them was the truth or not. They just thought the police coerced her into making the confession. For some reason, the Hispanic men and women on the jury were skeptical of police. I guess they've had bad experiences with them in the past."

Jones also noticed that "the Durans are upper-class Hispanics. Most of the jury weren't in their social circles. They couldn't relate to a lady with that kind of money and free time leaving her infant so long in a maid's care and then going off to a social function."

It seemed the jurors were also thinking about their households — Jones said about half of them had their own maids. Still others were remorsefully recalling their own pasts. "What [Cuca] did was intentional," Jones said. "But it was from frustration and could have happened to anyone. How many people are aware of how dangerous shaking a child can be? Most of us on the jury learned this for the first time at the trial. Think of those times you were young, you were babysitting, you got angry...some of us jurors were thinking, 'There but for the grace of God go I.'"

"It was very difficult," Jones remembered. "After we agreed she was guilty, some jurors actually wanted to go back on their decision, simply because she could get a lot of years in the state penitentiary. We finally agreed to the lesser charge of reckless endangerment. Because this being El Paso and most of the jurors being Hispanic, we already knew that, since she was from Mexico, if she got probation she could serve it in Juarez. Which basically means she'd get no punishment at all."

So the jury finally decided to give Cuca a suspended sentence with ten years probation administered by the Mexican authorities. She returned to Aunt Paulina's house in the slum near the mountains. For a time she worked near downtown Juarez, at an outdoor popsicle stand. Later she returned to her village in Zacatecas. Now, every few months, she travels to Juarez with her mother, to buy second-hand clothes to take back and sell to her townspeople.

As for the Durans, they have since left the home where Michelle died — friends say Diana couldn't bear living among the memories of that hot Friday afternoon in June.

Since then, it has become a violation of federal law to hire an undocumented maid. The new policy hasn't changed El Paso much, though. Young women from the interior still cross the river without papers; they still get jobs cleaning houses and minding kids. They still make the same money for the same hard work, still cloister themselves from the Border Patrol, still yearn for their weekends off. And still, undoubtedly, get frustrated with the endless squalling of kids who aren't theirs.

As for Cuca, attorney Anchondo got a call from her a couple of years ago. She was in Juarez and wanted to know if there was any way she could return to El Paso legally. He couldn't help her — she has a criminal record, and to get caught now by Immigration would almost surely land her in federal prison.

But no matter. There'll be others to take her place. "People on the border have always had maids and always will," says jury foreman Jones. "It's just something that goes with the territory." He remembers the final minutes of Cuca's trial and sentencing. As she rose to leave the court, several jurors surrounded her and shook her hand. They wished her luck and entreated her to use her head, be careful in the future.

Then one Hispanic woman came up. It seems this juror had three or four children herself, and she needed a maid to live in her home, do housework, care for the kids.

She offered Cuca the job.

Irma's Story: The Life of An Illegal Alien

All afternoon the Spanish radio newscaster rattled on about the raid at the Chicago & North Western station at Armitage and Ashland. The arrested passengers were heading up to places like Highland Park, to polish the silver and trim the lawns.

"Shit," I thought, "she's going to have to find some other way to get there if she ever goes job hunting again."

Not that she would, probably. Not after the luck we had with that $32 "Situation Wanted" ad we put in the Northern Suburbs-targeted classified section of the *Chicago Tribune*. "Listen," I'd told her, "if there's anyone with enough room and money to hire a live-in with two kids, they'll be up there. So we'll write this ad fancy, elegant...we won't even use abbreviations."

Even the Trib ad-taker lady was impressed with the language: "sterling character, hardworking to a fault, impeccable references" — it sounded like the third floor at *Upstairs Downstairs*.

The sad thing was that it was all true.

We got two calls: one from a Jewish art dealer who only liked German housekeepers, the other from a gentleman who said he was masturbating in the shower.

We wouldn't have gotten even those if we'd told the *Trib* ad lady to insert "wetback."

My friend — I'll call her Irma — didn't swim a river to get here — she flew in from Colombia on a jet, carrying a six-month tourist visa. Circumstances, though, have conspired to transform her into an honorary Mexican.

Irma looks like your generic south-of-the-border poor immigrant woman: stocky body; wide, Indian face; the kind of luxuriant coarse black hair that doesn't take kindly to home permanents. When she visits me she sits on the sofa with her baby and looks stolid and ordinary and unobtrusive. Ditto for her conversation. "A simple woman," says my friend from the Illinois Job Service. "A real employment problem with those two kids," she adds with a seasoned Job Service eye. "But at least she's clean."

To really know Irma, you'd have to hang around her long enough to catch her without shoes or slacks or support stockings. Then you'd see her feet swollen and twisted with bunions, her calves shot with varicose veins that make your eyes throb looking at them. These are the limbs of a woman who's spent the better part of her life on her feet, serving other people's meals, doing other people's laundry, other people's floors and ironing, making other people's beds, washing other people's dishes, caring for other people's babies.

That she does all these things marvelously is no sign of how much her life's work depresses her. She calls me up late at night sometimes, when all the work is done, and tells me how she despairs that her life will never change for the better. When she's really down, she says she's going to walk into the Immigration and Naturalization Service offices, turn herself in, and beg for mercy.

I calm her down and tell her if she'd come over on a boat instead of a plane, in some other century, she'd be one of the heroines of American history — the upwardly striving indentured servant women, the female factory operatives who struggled and made it into the middle class and beyond.

Small comfort. Now she's hounded by the threat of joblessness and the INS, living in constant fear of destitution and deportation. These days, she's scum, floating uselessly at the top of whatever it is they used to call the melting pot.

She says that's pretty much the way it's been most of her life, starting with childhood, which was spent in a straw hut with eight other kids in the Colombian countryside. Her father went to the mountains every day to burn wood into charcoal. Her mother carried chickens and eggs to the nearest city, and traded them for cast-off clothes for the children. Her father beat her mother unmercifully. He was just slightly gentler with her.

At age 14, she left home to escape him, and went to a nearby city to work as a domestic servant. At first she didn't take criticism well — she used to quit her job whenever the master or mistress screamed at her. But she found a boss who didn't scream much, and stayed for two years until she found herself bored and thinking of big-city life. But her boss wouldn't accept her resignation, and upped her salary. Her mother was pleased and ordered her to stay.

She had a boyfriend — a guy she enjoyed talking with — but the boss was strict and didn't allow it. So they said they were getting married, and the boss smiled as she spoke to her fiance. The credulous boyfriend even set a wedding date in a faraway city. They eloped to there, leaving mother and boss far behind.

She promptly told the boyfriend to get lost.

"I'd never get married," Irma tells me, "not after seeing how my father beat my mother the way he did."

So she was 16, working at a rooming house inhabited by young male college students. She did all their washing, ironing, cooking, and cleaning; they spied on her in the bathroom and in the shower and when she got undressed at night. She stayed there for years and it began to bother her that she'd never been to school and was illiterate. When she was about 22, she learned to read, and to write in a slow, halting way. She could do this, but at the age of 27 she was still making the beds of the young male college students.

She was, by Latin standards, a spinster, yet she loved children and looked longingly at women with their babies.

One of the roomers, an electrical engineering student, was 19 years old and wild. He used to chase her around and expose himself, laughing and beckoning. She said he was like an animal and used to rip her clothes off; when she got pregnant he was terrified and said she must get an abortion or his parents would no longer pay for his studies. She didn't get an abortion and didn't tell anybody who the father was, and had to live the entire time of her pregnancy in the rooming house with him around without anybody knowing what was going on; and he still ripped her clothes off her into her eighth month. She walked around pregnant feeling like the walking dead, like her life was over from the shame of it. She walked to the hospital by herself one day and had the baby with little pain.

"But I wouldn't have married that boy," she says, "even if he'd offered to. For one thing, I was considered his social inferior. And he repudiated his child — I said, 'To hell with you, the baby won't have your last name, don't worry, and I wouldn't lower myself to take a penny from you.'"

Later she earned her living bathing and dressing and giving medicine to an old man who was dying. Then the son of the dead man took ill himself. He'd left his job as a journalist, sold his gentleman's farm and his wife's portrait photography business to join cousins in the United State and seek greater fortune. He'd found nothing better than a job in a metal factory, returned disappointed to Colombia, and later developed fatal cancer in his nose, which everybody said came from working in the metal factory. His wife decided to take him back to the United States for the best medical treatment. They asked Irma to come along and be the nurse. She did, but after a few months, the man died.

Irma's six-month tourist visa expired. Meanwhile, having spent the family fortune on doctors, the deceased's wife got a job in a factory. Her teenage son began working in an Uptown roller rink, adopting the manners, dress, and speech of Puerto Ricans, who are U.S. citizens. One of these days, he'll probably marry a Puerto Rican girl who will love him and not charge him the $1,500 black market rate that Puerto Ricans command for marrying illegal Latin aliens whom they don't love.

Irma's services were no longer needed.

On the door of a Spanish grocery, she saw an ad placed by an Anglo couple with two children. The parents both worked and the wife was out of the house full-time. They hired her to be the housekeeper, one day a week off, room and board for herself and her little girl, $60 a week.

At first she considered herself lucky.

Though there were plenty of Spanish-speaking neighbors, the area was still too sparsely settled by them to attract the attention of the INS agents. The husband and wife (let's call them Kristin and Greg) she always addressed respectfully as *Doña* Kristi and *Don* Gregorio. The *Don* and *Doña* were *simpático* — they had adopted a Mexican infant, they lived modestly but comfortably, had a house full of fresh fruits and vegetables, books in Spanish, and mail from organizations like the Southern Poverty Law Center and Amnesty International. Doña Kristi had once run an English-language storefront school in Pilsen for illegal aliens. Her tuition had been so sympathetically low that the school quickly folded.

Whenever Doña Kristi needed a maid, she would put out the word on Hispanic grocery store bulletin boards or through the inchoate immigrant grapevine. That's how she got her previous maid, Tomasa, an illegal Mexican who eventually found a Puerto Rican to marry and sponsor her for permanent residency and freedom from the life of a domestic. Doña Kristi had all sorts of ideas for Irma. She sent Irma's daughter, by now five years old, to the same expensive private school that her older son attended. Doña Kristi had a degree in child psychology and spent time with the older son, helping him pore over thick coffee-table tomes while he memorized the paintings of the great masters and various styles of French provincial and Chippendale antiques. She criticized Irma for not allowing her little girl to play in the streets, for teaching her housework. She encouraged Irma to read the original Spanish version of *One Hundred Years of Solitude* instead of magazines like *Cosmopolitano*. She didn't allow Irma to speak any English in her house, since her own children were to become bilingual through domestic immersion.

At night, after 12 hours of housekeeping and babysitting, Irma was usually too tired to listen to her English-language cassette tapes. And on her one day a week off, she took to socializing with Guillermo, a Mexican who lived right across the street.

Guillermo said he was legal, but who knows? He said he'd made a marriage of convenience to the niece of Patty, his 60-year-old Chicana landlady, who was from El Paso and whose entire family was secure in its U.S. citizenship. Well, sometimes he said he was divorced, and he talked to Irma about marriage. But he was perpetually red faced from drink, perpetually propositioning even Irma's closest women confidantes. He would introduce her to his male pals with, "This is Irma. She's everybody's friend." And he used say her little girl was too aggressive, too undisciplined, too Americanized. That Irma should beat her.

She wanted to tell him to go to hell. But then, what would she have to fall back on? Laundry, cooking, diapers, 6 a.m. to 9 at night. The contrast between that and Guillermo's Saturdays at the movies and his evening caresses equaled something she tried to tell herself was love.

The first time Irma got pregnant by Guillermo, Doña Kristi and

Don Gregorio found an abortion clinic in the Loop, a place she'd never been before because she was terrified of INS agents roaming the streets of unknown places. The abortion was arranged and executed so quickly that Guillermo didn't find out until afterward.

For months, Irma said she thought about how she'd killed a little soul. She felt suicidal and prayed to God and the Virgin for forgiveness.

One day she was walking and a man, Bill, from Cicero, called out to her from his car and invited her for a drive that night. They went to the park and she valiantly conducted the entire date in English. Bill saw her into the house, held her little girl in his lap, left, and was never heard from again.

Doña Kristi said Irma would never get a citizen to marry her and give her residency papers because she acted sullen with men, turned them off. She should seek therapy, Doña Kristi said.

The second time she got pregnant Guillermo said, "I confess. I'm living with my landlady. So get rid of it."

Doña Kristi and Don Gregorio assumed that's just what she'd do, especially after they told her they couldn't afford to keep a house-keeper with two kids. For weeks it grew inside her and she struggled with Yellow Pages listings and listened to all the Spanish radio public service announcements. On the final day preceding her appointment at the abortion clinic, she found an organization that hooked her up with a Mexican woman in Little Village. The woman said she'd take in a pregnant woman and a six-year-old girl.

"It was an act of God," said Irma.

Doña Kristi cried.

At the prenatal clinic, they asked her how old she was. She said she didn't know because she'd been born in a hut and her birth had never been registered. "Could you be about 40?" asked the nurse. Irma shrugged and they arranged for high-risk, older-mother amnio-centesis. ("You're not a day over 35," I protested. "But I *feel* so old," she shrugged.)

The amniocentesis indicated the baby was a boy. "That's good," Irma said. "Because if it were a girl, I'd abort her."

"But what about her little soul?" I asked.

"Life here is hell for women anyway," she answered.

She named the baby an impossibly Anglo-Saxon name, some-thing like Scott. He is an American citizen, but that doesn't help much, since American-born children can't sponsor permanent residency for their foreign families until they reach majority.

Things were hard in Little Village. The woman Irma lived with, Beatriz, had been here legally for ten years, and her two girls were born in Chicago. Beatriz and her husband were doing pretty well. She supplemented his factory job with her own, making $6.80 an hour plus overtime assembling some obscure gadget used in the innards of automobiles. But then Beatriz's husband divorced her and ran off to Mexico, leaving behind thousands of dollars in unpaid bills.

Beatriz couldn't really afford the $50 a week she was paying Irma to watch her two kids while she worked. There were weeks when she didn't have any overtime and had to borrow grocery money from her coworkers to feed seven mouths: hers, Irma's, the four kids', and Sofía's.

Beatriz found Sofía crying on 26th Street. Sofía's boss, a restaurant owner on 18th Street, had sent her one-way fare from Mexico, promising her $100 a week to care for his children. When she arrived, he refused to pay her anything and threatened to turn her in to Immigration if she complained.

Beatriz took Sofía in and let her sleep in the tiny bedroom with her two daughters. Irma, her son, and her daughter occupied another room so small that in a better side of town it would house nothing more than a personal library or an ironing board.

For months Irma looked for steady work; she redoubled her efforts after Guillermo gave her a parting gift of a phony green card. It's not really green, but that's what everyone calls the permanent residency document that employers ask for when you apply for a job and you're a foreigner. Guillermo had a friend who got it for him for $50 — that's $30 less than the going price on the street. As for her counterfeit Social Security card, Irma paid $40 to a woman she used to chat with at the grocery store.

Once she took the green card to a hotel near O'Hare, and Personnel asked her to sign a release permitting them to cross-check her registration number with the INS. It was damned if she did and damned if she didn't. So she did.

She left the house at 5:30 AM each day and caught a bus, then an el, then another bus, and got to work at 7:30. At 3:30 she went the other way around, two hours' worth. At work she had to clean one hotel suite every 30 minutes, and if she pushed the cleaning cart too slowly or left a dust mote on a night table, the black supervisors screamed at her. For 60 hours commuting and working per week, she took home $166 net. The old-timer maids, out-and-out illegal aliens, sneered. "You couldn't possibly be legal," they said. "Or why would you take such a shitty job?"

She was happy, though.

A month later, Personnel called her in and told her they'd been informed she was undocumented and that they regretted they couldn't take on any new illegals, what with all the old ones they already had. This was a large-scale enterprise, you see, and they didn't want to get in trouble should Congress pass the Simpson-Mazzoli immigration bill, which would make it a crime for an employer to hire illegals.

A storefront lawyer advised Irma to leave her house immediately and hide for a few days. Beatriz took all the names off the mailbox and told the kids not to answer the door to anybody they didn't know.

After that, when walking down the street or riding a bus, Irma started looking carefully at everybody, trying to figure out if they could be INS agents. It was hopeless though — the agents work in plainclothes.

Then the House of Representatives passed Simpson-Mazzoli, which Irma and her friends knew simply as *La Amnistía*. The day after the vote, she and Beatriz were sitting around the kitchen table waiting to hear the upcoming news about what the Senate would decide. Meanwhile, a Spanish radio commentator was discussing the ins and outs of the law.

He said the Senate and House were arguing — possibly without resolution — about whether to grant amnesty in this country to 1.5 to 3 million illegal aliens (of a total of 3 to 15 million living here). They couldn't agree, either, on how long you'd have to have lived here to get amnesty: since 1982? 1980? Or as early as 1978? In any case, the House said, to get in under the wire, immigrants would have to know American history, civics, and English. Irma wondered if she'd have to take a test. If so, would she know the answers? She wondered if this new law might just be a trick to get her to register with INS and then deport her. She thought maybe it would be less trouble for her to just go back home. Except that in Colombia, kids like hers wouldn't be of the social class that could afford to drink milk.

"How are your varicose veins doing?" asked Beatriz.

"Not so well," Irma said. "You know, that operation I once had to fix them was the most frightening thing that's ever happened to me. They gave me anesthesia and I dreamed that Death came to me in the form of a choice. I was supposed to pick only one word, which I would have to say over and over for all eternity. I chose the word, but it was the wrong one. So wrong! But then I had to repeat this monstrously ugly sound over and over. Over and over. Forever! Just remembering that dream terrifies me!"

"Was it in English or Spanish?" asked Beatriz.

"Don't even make me think about it," said Irma.

"Where am I going to get money for groceries next week?" said Beatriz. *"Dios mío,* if I end up having to sell this house, where will you all go?"

The radio was playing a maudlin ranchero.

"Yeah...things are hard," added Beatriz. *"Duro, duro."*

"Duro, duro!" wailed the song.

"Did you hear that?" said Irma.

They looked at each other and burst out laughing. Then they waited for the news to come on.

Epilogue

Two years after this was written, Congress passed the 1986 Immigration Reform and Control Act — *"La Amnistía"* that Irma was hoping for. The cut-off date was 1982, which meant Irma and her daughter qualified. But David didn't. He was Irma's new Mexican boyfriend. David had been a teacher in Mexico; now he eked out a living teaching Spanish part-time at a Chicago community center, and selling cotton candy at flea markets.

David was illegal, but he was gentle with the children, never got drunk and never beat Irma. They had a daughter and got married, without knowing whether he would ever be able to live openly in the U.S. Later, though, amnesty was extended to the illegal spouses of people like Irma. She and David then had a second daughter; at this writing there are four children. Irma is still cleaning houses and find-ing life very difficult. By law, she, David, and her oldest daughter still don't qualify for benefits, like food stamps, that make things easier for the native born and permanent resident poor. A couple of years ago the family started going weekends to the neighborhood Salvation Army to get extra food and clothes. David and Irma found the Army's brand of evangelism comforting, and both are now fundamentalist Christians who spend most of their spare time holding religious services in their tiny living room and proselytizing, in Spanish, through the streets of Little Village.

Meanwhile, Beatriz moved away — she married a black man she met at her factory, and they took their kids to the suburbs. As for Sofía, she came to America too late to qualify for "La Amnistía." She left Beatriz' and Irma's home long ago, but is likely still illegal, and probably still someplace in Chicago, though no one knows for sure.

— 1984

Salvador

I met Socorro while I was doing an article describing the typical Juarez family's efforts to eat on a food budget of $25 a week. When I started the research, Mexican groceries were running at least half what they cost in U.S. supermarkets, the peso's value was slipping daily, and the government had withdrawn its "people's" subsidies on cooking oil. Leftist political parties and public think tanks, meanwhile, were issuing lugubrious pronouncements about how the average working class Mexican family, in order to consume the minimum requirements of calories, protein and vitamins each week, would have to use 100 percent of its income for food.

The average family — if it was paying its light bill and opting to wear clothes — obviously wasn't spending everything on groceries. My piece was thus about malnutrition among most of the adults and children of Juarez, and my investigative plan was to sit in working class kitchens, from morning till night, noting on a steno pad everything that went into the families' mouths and how much it cost. I would then phone the data in to some evangelical Christian dietitians in East Texas who'd been to Juarez once to set up storefront churches, and who'd developed an academic interest in quantifying their new flock's iron deficiency anemias.

Actually, Socorro wasn't my first contact. I started with the Zavala family, up in the hills of colonia Mariano Escobedo. The mother, Chela, had been recommended to me by her neighbor Catalina, who regularly sneaks into El Paso to clean the house of one of my neighbors. One weekday morning, early, I packed a lunch for myself and took a public van up through the gullies leading to the Zavalas' one-room, dirt-floor adobe hut.

Chela and her husband have four daughters, ages three to nine. Mr. Zavala, a squat, quiet and good natured man ("without vices," Chela says), is a master bricklayer who works steady, six days out of seven, for $46 a week. Chela is thin and has bulging doe eyes that hardly ever meet your gaze directly. She wears old, prim clothes and her only indulgence seems to be a home permanent that makes her look like Harpo Marx. The girls are beautiful, sweet and spindly. The family lives crammed between two beds, an old armoire, a World War II-era refrigerator with no power, another one that works, and a black and white console TV, on top of which sits the vitamin tonic of the eldest daughter, who was recently diagnosed as being 13 pounds underweight. The day I was there, she lay in one of the beds sick, thin-necked, white like a swan, and restless with fever.

The two preschoolers stayed home too, and all day I watched them and their mother buying, cooking and eating food. My notebook became a jumble: "cornflakes w/ milk and sugar for kids; market Sundays 6,000 pesos/week (24 dollars); one kilo ground meat, 1/2 kilo cheese, noodles, six cokes a day from corner store, three lbs. lard/week; beans; she's out of tortillas and bread because it's Friday; lunch rice fried in lard w/ onion and garlic; no more canned tomatoes, too late in week; outhouse. no shower. outside water tap OK now — no water in summer."

By mid-afternoon it was hot, the girls were drowsy and quiet, and Chela and I had time to talk of other things. She is a sweet, meek woman, not interested in crossing town, much less the border. She has no desire to work in a maquila — "I want to be at home for my girls," she says — and though they've lived in Juarez for years and can see the skyscrapers of El Paso from their front yard, no one in the family, not even Mr. Zavala, has ever been there.

"They're stuck in that shack, living that pathetic life, because they have too many kids and won't hustle," sniffed their neighbor Catalina once, as she bustled around a shiny U.S. kitchen. Back in the colonia, in a corner of the hut with a rickety table and the old refrigerator, Chela agreed. "We're not ambitious," she said, shamefaced. Later, just as abashed, she apologized for the large number of children she'd borne. *"La familia pequeña vive mejor,"* Chela said, echoing the

Mexican government's national contraception campaign slogan. She'd learned this little jingle from TV and from the *promotoras* — ladies who trudge through the colonias like distaff census workers, knocking on doors and cajoling women like Chela to use birth control pills and other supplies paid for by the government and the Agency for International Development. By the time Chela learned the promotoras' lessons, though, it was too late. "Four is too many," she said ruefully. "But *ni modo!* Now what can we do?"

Then I found Socorro, who seemed altogether different. I met her through Lupe and Reyna. They were the *chavas,* or chicks, as their male *compañeros* called them, from the Trotskyist Revolutionary Workers Party, better known as the PRT. The PRT was supporting a Marxist squatter group's candidates for the legislature, organizing out in the colonias, and Lupe told me about this woman they'd run into.

"Her name's Socorro and she's a pretty militant housewife," Lupe said. "When we marched downtown in the women's Empty Pots and Pans demonstration to protest rising food prices, she got up and made a speech. When someone seizes a piece of land and the cops come and bang heads, Socorro's head is out there on the line. Go sit with her all day. You'll see the problems working class families face."

So I did. One early weekday morning I took a bus from the downtown Cathedral to Bella Vista, the neighborhood fronting the river across from the Amtrak station in El Paso. Bella Vista is just west of downtown and is the oldest workers' colonia in Juarez. Here the streets are named after fragrant flowers and precious metals, and it's said that during the Vietnam war, when the Mariscal whorehouses hopped with the traffic from Fort Bliss, Violetas and Aluminio were dotted with mulatto children. But that time has already passed, the *negritos* of Bella Vista are grown up and gone, and lately, in the still unsettled spaces between older homes, squatters have invaded and erected new ones. Socorro is one such recent arrival — with the help of a community group, she seized a small plot of land, legalized the title to it, and started building.

My first impression: she has a nice house — at least, compared to the hovel atmosphere at Chela's. Socorro's place is fresh and woody, with pine roof beams and good cinder block walls. The one room measures 12 feet by 18, the floor isn't dirt, but smooth and level cement, and not only are there two beds, a stove, a refrigerator and two TV's, there's plenty of space separating these objects. After Chela's, everything about Socorro's seems reassuring. The children — there are only three of them — look hale and sturdy. Water runs freely from an indoor tap. Even though it's Friday, there are tall stacks of tortillas, and the refrigerator holds packages of ground beef. The husband is off in Fort Worth, making good money, sending home $75 a week. Here there is gumption, consumption. When I first see it, it feels manageable, livable. A relief.

The children eat their breakfast — eggs, milk and bread — and I happily write it all down while they leave for school. Faster, much faster than at Chela's, Socorro totes up her week's grocery list for me, along with the exact price of each commodity. She is medium height and vaguely stocky, with the kind of thick hair that has no curl but which still stands up airily, like an animal's winter coat. Unlike Chela, she looks at me directly. Especially when she recounts facts, such as exactly how many grams of sugar per week she usually buys.

Soon we've finished our work and there's nothing special to do. The youngest child, a preschooler, hears the street spiel of an itinerant candy vendor and begs for a treat. Socorro refuses; the little girl opens the fridge and dunks her finger into an open can of tomato sauce. While I'm writing this down, Jose Luis Cervantes walks in.

He's a tough old coot, dark, maybe 60 years old, battered and very handsome, like an old sailor who somehow ended up landlocked in the Chihuahua desert. He's the head of the *Alianza de Colonos Populares*, the group that helped Socorro seize the land for her new home. So now she "militates" with them, and meanwhile, the Trotskyists in the PRT are doing their electoral work with the Alianza. Later, Reyna and Lupe tell me the Alianza consists of Jose Luis and a bunch of neighborhood women. He lives near Socorro's, alone, in a tiny hut, painted with all sorts of slogans and graffiti, shaped like his body and just a bit bigger — a sort of ultra-left, adobe sarcophagus.

Jose Luis, it turns out, is a long time local radical; he achieved international notoriety back in 1976 when El Paso and Juarez leftists protesting the death of a young Mexican immigrant at downtown's "Black Bridge" clashed with the Border Patrol. During the melee Jose Luis was arrested and booked as an illegal alien; he told INS officials that if they didn't release him he'd order 20,000 of his Mexican followers to storm the U.S. It never happened (he was eventually merely deported); and now he still seems irritated by gringos. I can hardly understand a word he says, though my Spanish usually suffices even in the colonias. Jose Luis wants to intimidate. But maybe not just me.

The conversation goes like this:

1. As a journalist, I should be exposing a corrupt Mexican drug dealer who is now living in El Paso. ("Who is he? What's his name?" I ask, flipping a page in my notebook and poising my pen. "That's for you to find out," he snickers.)

2. Socorro should comb her hair.

3. The revolution will rid Mexico of economic intervention into her sovereignty.

4. Women are all lazy these days. Because they don't can tomatoes and make tortillas by hand like they used to. Now they even buy bologna. Terrible for the kids!

5. Women should not go around pregnant all the time — much prettier to have a flat belly! And why do women marry men by force instead of by love? If you don't love the guy, just let him leave! (He says he has 25 children by six wives, and has not lived with any of them for years.)

6. Socorro should get her truck repaired immediately.

7. She should comb her hair.

After Jose Luis leaves, we talk politics. Socorro is very direct with facts, almost aggressive — as though she'd like to push you over with them. When I ask her why she's a militant, for instance, she reaches under a bed, pulls out a big cardboard box stuffed with snapshots and holds one to my face. It shows the mud hut she and the family lived in, in another colonia, before she seized the land we're on now. Socorro caresses this photo, says she wants to show it to their kids when they're old enough to appreciate how far the family has progressed.

But when she says "socialism" and I ask "What is socialism?" she says she doesn't know exactly; she's still learning. With such uncertainties, Socorro is more veiled, less direct, even sheepish. But soon she retrieves the facts, and they are these:

1. She doesn't know what socialism is, exactly, but

2. She *will* learn.

These are the facts. They do my notebook no good, but armed with them, Socorro is aggressive again.

She tells me about herself. She's 27 years old and her husband is 39. She was raised on a *ranchito* in downstate Chihuahua and is the oldest of 15 children. She is terrified of cancer and of diabetes; both diseases, she says, run in her family, and her mother died from diabetes (she begs me to bring her little envelopes of Sweet 'n Low so she won't get it). Her mother was always ill, so it fell to Socorro to raise the siblings. She married at age 13 — he was 25 then — and she thought getting married and leaving the house and all the younger brothers and sisters would make life easier. And now? Well, OK, she hasn't had as many children as her mother did. So in a sense life is easier. On the other hand, the kids she's got now are hers, not her mother's. And that makes things even harder.

Then there's her husband. "He's coming home tomorrow and I'm very nervous," she says. "When we got married I was just a kid. I grew up with him. He's good to me and the children. Believe me, I'd never let a man hit me anyway (I'd hit him back!). He's been sympathetic to my activity with the *Alianza*. But he gets into these moods…he gets quiet…then he goes around with other women. Yet he comes back and lies with me, and says he loves me. But it drives me crazy! Around Christmas, he was going with another woman and I found out. We fought so much about it that he decided it would be better for him to go for awhile to the 'other side.' That was six months ago, and he's been sending me money every week, regular. Now he's coming home tomorrow. He says he wants to try again with me. But sometimes I think it's just for the kids' sake."

She goes to the mattress again and pulls out a notebook. It's filled with poems — handwritten poems, pages and pages of them, only a bit misspelled despite her third grade education. They are all dedicated to her husband, all about how she yearns that they will finally love and comprehend one another. The poems are done in a Loretta Lynne sort of style; they would be very nice set to music. Socorro wants to talk with me about love, about why men and women can't love each other with real understanding. When her husband returns, she wants everything between them to be perfect, absolutely perfect. But it's no use — she knows already that in a matter of time, the rancor in her will explode and spoil everything between them. She starts to cry quietly. There's a knock at the door.

It's the PRT girls. They've come to read Lupe's draft article for the party's national newspaper, about the Empty Pots and Pans rally in downtown Juarez that Socorro participated in. It seems the unique thing about this protest was that, purely spontaneously, some of the women who marched grabbed the microphone and spoke ad lib to the crowd. When men are around, they never do things like that. Socorro was one of the speakers, and now Lupe wants her to repeat what she said so they can publish it in the paper.

"I can't remember any of it," demurs Socorro. Lupe tries to help, pulls out her notebook: "Well, you talked about how hard it is to feed your family on the minimum wage. Right? How about some details about that?" Socorro gets her humble look. She nods, agrees; but she's downcast and mute. Lupe insists. "Well, like what you were telling Debbie. Like, you used to go out to restaurants but now you don't anymore? Because you can't afford it?" More hems and haws and silence. So Lupe reads what she's already written anyway — long passages about the impossible price of cooking oil and chicken; laments for our children's futures; brave urgings: Not to despair! Don't give up! Organize and struggle!

Socorro nods perfunctory agreement.

Then they ask if the Party can use her house today at 6 p.m. To conduct a poll watcher class.

"Well I — I don't know," Socorro says. "I've just been feeling so nervous lately. I've been crying a lot."

"About what?" says Lupe (Reyna sits there with her nose scrunched up.)

Socorro looks like they just asked her again about her Pots and Pans speech.

"Oh well, everybody cries at times," Lupe says. "Listen, we have to go. So what about it? Your house, I mean? Because it'd be really hard to cram everyone into Jose Luis' hut. So can we use your house? Yeah? OK — see you at six."

They rush out.

The door opens again. It's the kids, home from school for lunch. Socorro invites me to put aside the brown bag I brought for myself and join them. I decline, she insists. So I do, and soon I'm trying to eat and write at the same time. There's a lot of writing to do because there's a lot of food: tortillas, a stew of spaghetti noodles and sliced hot dogs, limeade, salsa made with tomatoes and fiery little green chilies. While the children eat, Socorro spoons salsa into her mouth and absently pours salt onto the tablecloth. As though they were filterless cigarettes, she raps her fingers in the salt, then licks them, over and over. Meanwhile, she's chain smoking real cigarettes — the cheap, rank Mexican kind. I note it all in my steno book — everything that goes into her mouth.

Suddenly I'm stricken with doubts. I realize that by eating Socorro's food I may have corrupted my research. After all, in this poor family, everything is supposed to count: every calorie, every mouthful, every mouth. Does mine, then? Who am I in this home? An extraordinary expense? A guest? Or what?

The children leave again and Socorro brings me out of my troubled musings. "I need to talk to you," she says. "About the crying."

She gets into these moods, she says. Thinks about her husband, about other things, about everything. And it drives her crazy. When it happens — one of these spells — it helps a lot to go walking. Walk to the middle of town, and if there's a demonstration, it cheers her up to get in the middle of it, talk to people, yell.

Last year, she says, it was bad. Once she got into one of her crying-wandering-the-streets spells and took 25 sleeping pills. She did this on a Sunday and when she woke up she thought it was still Sunday but it turned out to be Thursday. Now she's in a mood to do it again. That's what it is, a mood. And when you get it you can't help it.

There's no one to talk to. Jose Luis and Lupe and Reyna, they all think that, because she goes and gets her head cracked open by the cops while defending a squatter family's right to a piece of land — because she grabs the microphone and yells things, they think she's strong. But it's a lie. Really, she's weak.

I don't know what to say. I stare down at my notes, nonplused.

She weeps again quietly. "I want to go to Salvador," she says.

"Salvador?" I echo, mystified. "Who's Salvador?"

She answers by telling me the history of her fecundity.

The first child, Esteban, she had at age 15. He's 12 now and still alive. The second, Jazmin, is 11. The third — it was born with what the doctors called "cardiac insufficiency", and after 40 days it died. The next third was a little girl, born healthy. Then, there was a fourth child, Lucy, the one who just had her finger in the tomato sauce. Lucy was born three months premature, before the third child had her second birthday.

One day, Socorro went to the hospital to nurse Lucy. She left the other kids with their grandmother. The two-year-old, whose picture she shows me, loved bananas. The sisters and brother would take their coins to the corner grocery store and buy candy, but the little girl never wanted anything but bananas. On this day, she toddled into the market, bought a banana, and coming back across the street, she fell behind a truck. It backed up and fractured her skull. People on the street screamed to the driver. Confused, he drove forward. This crushed the child's lungs.

She was taken to the hospital, regained consciousness and cried lustily. The doctors said she would live. But Socorro knew it wasn't true. The police wanted her to come down to the station to swear out the accident report. She thought, "I can't go, I'll never see this child alive again." "No, no," everyone said. "She'll be OK — go." When Socorro got back, her daughter was dead.

She shows me the funerary snapshots, in color. The little girl's head is bruised but beautiful, her eyes half open, the face with its smooth opalescence of infant death.

Now Socorro had three children again.

"Everyone said forget her," she says, "but I can't. She used to get out of bed at night when it was very hot. And she would lie right here on the floor, because the floor is cooler. I'd get up and put her back in her bed. For a year after she died, I got up to move her every night. I'd shake my husband awake, crying that I couldn't find her. He'd say, 'Stop it. She's gone.'

"After my little girl was killed," Socorro continues, "I denied the existence of God. I said, 'Why couldn't this happen to some other mother? Or to one of those old, sick, hungry people you see begging in the streets, with their lives almost over anyway? Why did God want *my* baby?' But my mother told me I was selfish to ask."

"A year later, we were at the Black Bridge. We'd just come back from the park and we had a toy inner tube. Esteban wanted to swim in the river and I said, 'No *m'ijo*, it's too dangerous.' But my husband said, 'Let him go in.' He did, and he got caught by a current and disappeared."

"In those moments I realized that God was punishing my egoism. Suddenly, I was completely resigned to Him. I said, 'God, I believe in You and I accept that You've taken my son. I only ask one thing: that You not keep his body in the river for a week before letting it float, as usually happens. But please, God, give me my son's body today.'"

"And then Esteban floated up and they got him and put him on the river bank. And he regained consciousness."

"And since then, I haven't denied the existence of God."

Then she tells me about another fourth child, this one a hard delivery. The doctors said Socorro's womb was "filled with water" and "drowned the baby's lungs." During labor they told her it wouldn't live. They wanted to do a Caesarean. She demanded a local spinal anesthetic so she would be conscious during the birth — she wanted to see the baby while it was still alive. But the drug had no effect and she could feel everything — all the pain, the knives cutting in her flesh and womb. It was horrible! She knew though that if she gave even a groan, they'd knock her out. So she was silent, and she saw them take the moving baby out of her.

"Suddenly," Socorro says, "it dawned on me. God is in agreement with the National Family Planning Program. *La Familia Pequeña Vive Mejor*, and He wants me to have only three children! So if I have a fourth one and it lives, that only means that one of the older children will die in order to make the fourth the third again." Having realized this, she told the doctors that as long as they were cutting her open, to take the opportunity to sterilize her. She said that and screamed. They gave her a general anesthetic, and when she woke up, the fourth baby was gone and her tubes were severed.

She begins crying quietly again, but searches for the thought that comforts her. The Trotskyists have asked her to go down to Mexico City with them at the end of this month! To attend their pre-election national convention. They'll pay the bus fare and everything. She thinks her husband will permit it. It should be exciting!

Then suddenly, she says it again: "I want to go to Salvador. El Salvador."

At first I think I understand. "Oh!" I say. "You mean the *country!*"

"Yes," she says. "El Salvador. What do you think of it?"

Again I'm at a loss. I have no idea what she wants to know. I try talking about how the revolution there is different from the one in Nicaragua — the classes are so much more polarized. Then I don't know if she knows "polarized." Or cares. I repeat some things I heard at a forum given in Chicago by a diplomat representing the FMLN: about how in the guerrilla areas, the communities run everything, and in the running of everything, there's inspiration for what life will be like after a revolution, life in its freshness and richness. I look at her and feel as though I'm reading a souvenir menu from some restaurant she doesn't go to anymore, or worse, where she never went, even before the peso was devalued.

"I want to go there," she says, "To Salvador."

"To Salvador…." I echo.

"Yes, Salvador. Because the people there are so poor! Poorer than us!"

I try to be realistic. "What about Guatemala?" I say. "If the PRT pays your way to Mexico City, you can easily go there. Or just go to the Mexican border — to Chiapas, where all the Guatemalan refugees are in the camps. You could check conditions, do political work against repression in Guatemala, against Mexico's repression of the refugees. You actually could do *that*."

"Oh no, not the Guatemalans," she says. "No, no. They're so ugly."

"Ugly," I say. I try to merely echo. But she must hear something more, because she draws herself up, direct, aggressive.

"*Look*," she says. "Look. My family doesn't really suffer. We have this house, we have fuel in the winter for heat. My husband sends money, we have a *washing machine!* And we have enough to eat. Yes, we could easily feed another mouth."

"A fourth child — that's what I want! But besides myself, I must think of my country and of God, and how neither wants me to bear another baby. Then, after God and country, I think of myself again. So I won't make a child from *my* body. I'll get someone else's.

"So you understand. Guatemalans are *not* good looking. But the Salvadorans — they're so handsome! I'd adopt one from there. And it would be a beautiful child. Beautiful! That's what I yell when I go to the demonstrations. When I bang the pots and pans. I scream, 'I want a son! I want a son from Salvador!' Understand? From Salvador!"

And by how she puts it, I know this isn't about political marches, calories, hunger, family planning, or any other of the narrow things of uncertainty and wordless humility. Socorro's facts sprawl too wide for the columns of my steno pad. So I close it and cap my pen. Her tears dry and we talk. Soon it will be six o'clock and the revolutionaries will be at the door. We wait for their knock, our fingers streaking salt on the kitchen table.

Abortion Stories on the Border

"Your period's late?" The clerk at Ciudad Juarez's Benavides Pharmacy offers a customer syringes of female hormones. "Inject this twice," she advises. Down the street, at the market where El Pasoans and tourists buy party piñatas, herbalists hawk bags of leaves and bark. "Guaranteed to bring on your period if you're less than three months overdue," one vendor says.

In Mexico, with few exceptions, abortion is a crime. State law governing the city of Juarez, for instance, declares that a woman convicted of having an illegal abortion can be imprisoned for as long as five years, and her abortionist for three.

Nevertheless, before the U.S. Supreme Court legalized abortion in 1973, American women flocked to Mexico to end their pregnancies. Black market abortions were easy to get then; and though most still offered today are medically risky, they remain available.

Texas already prohibits Medicaid funding of abortion and restricts techniques used to abort "viable fetuses" older than 20 weeks. After the Supreme Court ruled on the Webster case, Texas was considered one of 22 states likely to further limit or even outlaw abortion. Should this happen, the Mexican border may once again become an abortion underground option for many American women.

Elizabeth Canfield, a Planned Parenthood counselor in Albuquerque, New Mexico, worked from 1968 to 1971 with Clergy Counseling Service for Problem Pregnancies in Los Angeles. The group referred American women to abortionists in Mexican border cities, especially Juarez.

"Juarez had many abortionists," Canfield said. "Most were physicians; others were laypeople trained by doctors. They charged $160 to $200 to do an early abortion, and millions of dollars were being made. Everybody had relationships with the cop on the beat. Enormous payoffs were taking place — they couldn't conceive of the U.S. referrers not wanting a kickback."

A woman who went to Mexico for an abortion entered a James Bond world, Canfield says. "You needed to carry your money inside your bra. You couldn't ever say 'abortion,' just something like 'Liz sent me.'"

"Though some black market abortion providers were very humanitarian," Canfield says, "they were all doing it for the money." Even back-up services, like airlines, cleaned up — whether intentionally or not. She recalls, for instance, one U.S. travel agent who "didn't want to know anything about what we were doing when we made reservations through her. One day she called me and said, 'You won't believe this, but we received an award for selling the most three-day weekends to Mexico.' Her boss kept asking how it was that so many of her clients wanted to go there. She was mortified!" Canfield remembers.

After abortion was legalized in the United States, the Mexican black market dissolved. Mexican women of means, however, can still find doctors who will occasionally provide discreet early abortions, says Dr. Francisco Urango Vallarta, former director of the Autonomous University's medical school in Chihuahua City, about 225 miles beyond the border.

"It's illegal, of course, so no one is going to routinely do the procedure and thus earn a reputation as an abortionist," Urango says. "But occasionally, a doctor will, say, fall behind on his car payments. Then he may do one." The procedure of choice, Urango says, is the dilatation and curettage (D&C) procedure, scraping the pregnant patient's uterus under the pretext of checking for diseases. The D&C automatically causes abortion.

Many Mexican doctors who favor abortion rights but are reluctant to break the law refer their patients to U.S. clinics such as Reproductive Services in El Paso. Reproductive Services does 2,500 abortions annually, and a quarter of the patients are from Mexico. Most are middle- and upper-class women seeking medically safe abortions.

Those Mexican women with neither connections nor money to cross the border must rely on cheap home or drugstore remedies. As indigent American women did in the United States before abortion was legalized, many Mexicans trying to end their pregnancies drink tea made of herbs such as thyme, rue, or cedar bark, sold at herb markets. Or they use synthetic chemicals. At a Mexican pharmacy one doesn't need prescriptions to buy hormone injections and drugs to make the uterus contract so as to expel the fetus. If such measures aren't successful, a Mexican woman may apply caustic chemicals or pay midwives or nurses, nicknamed "stork scarers," to stick catheters through her cervix.

These methods are often ineffective and dangerous. The Mexican Social Security Institute reported almost 60,000 cases of abortion-related complications in 1988. Of those, at least 100 resulted in massive infections or hemorrhaging that led to death. Indeed, in Mexico, illegal abortion is considered the second most common cause of maternal mortality (after childbirth). Even so, the country's federal Health Secretariat estimates that at least 500,000 of the procedures are performed annually.

In Ciudad Juarez, Dr. Carlos Cano Vargas, Assistant Chief of Obstetrics and Gynecology at the city's General Hospital, believes many of the 350 miscarriages his department sees annually are really illegal abortions.

"But it's hard to prove," he says, "because everyone conceals it. The pharmacy drugs leave no traces. Infection can happen after a natural miscarriage too, so that's no proof either. You may see caustic chemical lesions or a catheter, but that's very rare. A woman can be on her death bed and usually won't admit anything. In six years I've seen only two cases of obvious abortions. For every verifiable one in Juarez, there are countless more covered up."

Delia is a pseudonym for a Juarez woman whose abortion would have gone unnoticed last year had it not been botched. The 26-year-old is the mother of three preschoolers; her husband is a "twin plant" factory worker, earning about $40 per week. When their youngest child was six months old, Delia found herself pregnant again. She is taciturn but matter-of-fact while describing what happened next.

"We couldn't afford another child, so I took hormone shots from the drugstore and rue tea from the herb market. Nothing worked. Then a friend told me about a nurse abortionist. For $350,000 pesos (at the time about $200) she put a catheter up me that she was going to remove next day. But at night I got such a high fever that my husband insisted I go to a clinic. If only I'd known how to take out the catheter! Because when the doctor saw it in me he got really mad and called the police. They came and interrogated me, but of course I wouldn't tell them where the nurse was.

"The police made the clinic detain me for three days. Later at the station I was interrogated again for four hours. Finally, the detectives left the room and I just walked out. I hid at my mother's house for a few days but the police never came back."

"Oh yes," Delia said, "it's very common for women here to get abortions. If you know the pharmacist you can get the injections, and there are lots of abortionists. A lot of my friends have had abortions. Most already have children."

Delia's abortion was reported in the local Mexican press — complete with her name and address — on the police blotter page, along with stories about gang leaders, robbers and rapists. She was never indicted, however.

"It is hard to prosecute these cases," shrugs State Police Chief Investigator Saul Oscar Osollo. Delia's was one of only about five abortions reported to the Juarez police each year, he said.

Some Mexican women with botched abortions are luckier than Delia — they make it to El Paso, where health care providers like Reproductive Services do mop-up duty. Once, says clinic director Patti Pagels, "We suctioned a woman's uterus and found rubber bands in it. The patient was from Juarez. We told her we weren't going to report it, but she wouldn't admit having done anything."

Another recent patient, a 17-year-old, "came in already 16 or 17 weeks pregnant. The lab work indicated she was perfectly healthy; but — this is how fast the infection sets in — next day when she returned, a faucet of green, rancid pus was coming out of her vagina. We immediately gave her 2000 milligrams of tetracycline. An hour later she was blue and shivering — she couldn't swallow and her temperature was 104.5. She ended up spending five days on antibiotics at Thomason (El Paso's county hospital)."

"She told us she'd gone to somebody in Juarez who'd stuck something up her. It scared me! I thought, 'What if she hadn't come here? How long would she have waited to tell her parents?'"

"Death from septic abortion is horrible," Pagels says. "My God, nobody should ever have to die like that."

Elizabeth Canfield, recalling her work two decades ago referring American women to Mexican abortionists, predicts that if abortions are outlawed in Texas, women will travel to other states where they remain legal. But if a change in the law results in ready availability of abortion in Mexican cities, Americans along the border may go south as they did in the past.

Canfield keeps in touch with a former Juarez abortionist. "He's now a law enforcement officer," she said. "He told me recently that if things ever get tough again in this country, he'll help us again.

— 1989

Abortion
Abecedarium

The following lists were gleaned from *Legal Medicine, Pathology and Toxicology*, a now out-of-print text written by New York City medical examiners, and filled with tips on how to determine, say, if a dismembered corpse dredged from a large river is a murder victim, or merely a suicide by drowning that later crossed paths with a steamship propeller.

Legal Medicine was considered *the* authority for coroners nationally during the 1930s, 40s and 50s, when abortion was illegal and, therefore, a forensic matter. Hence, Chapter 22 instructs the medical examiner on how to inspect a dead woman's uterus to decide, for example, whether she herself inserted the knitting needle that killed her, or if it was the work of an abortionist (the two acts carried different criminal classifications and penalties).

The book notes that in each year between 1937 and 1941, the authors performed autopsies on about 65 New York City women dead from known or presumed illegal abortions. Below are some of the things such women did, ate or inserted, as well as the particular ways they took sick and expired. These lists of invention and suffering — vaguely remembered women's folkways mixed with the new chemicals and commodities of the industrial revolution — follow little rhyme, and less reason. But they may soon have to be republished in modern coroners' manuals, and there seems no other way to order them than by the comforting canon of the alphabet.

Means

Aloe. Alum. Ammonia. Apiol. Bicycle riding. Bitter apple. Black hellebore. Borax. Camphor. Catheters. Colocynth. Cotton root bark. Croton oil. Darning needles. Ergot. Gamboge. Hot baths. Imitation oil of bitter almonds. Jumping up and down stairs. Laburnum. Lead. Lysol. Methyl salicylate. Nitrobenzol. Oil of nutmeg. Oil of savin (juniper). Oil of pennyroyal. Oil of rue. Oil of tansy. Oil of thyme. Oleander leaves and bark. Oxytocin. Phenol (carbolic acid). Quinine. Saffron. Salts of arsenic. Slippery elm sticks. Soapy water. Spanish fly (dried beetle, of the species *Cantharis vesicatoria*). Sponges. Turpentine. Umbrella ribs. Urethral sounds. White phosphorous (scraped from the tips of kitchen matches). Yew. Zinc sulfate (white vitriol).

Ends

Acute suppurative peritonitis. Ataxia. *Bacillus welchii* (resulting in gangrenous endometritis and myometritis in the uterus, turning it black red in color). Bronze-colored skin. Central nervous system depression. Chills. Coma. Convulsions. Death. Delirium. Dyspnea. Embolic lung abscesses. Excitement. Exuberant vegetations on the mitral, tricuspid and aortic valves. Fever. Gastroenteritis (severe). Hemorrhage from the uterus. Hemolytic *streptococcus*. Irregular breathing. Irritation of the kidney. Irritation of the bladder. Jaundice. Lacerations. Oil embolism. Perforated intestine (and other perforating wounds of the abdominal viscera). Perforating wounds of the uterus. Pulmonary air embolism. Purulent yellowish-green or grayish-brown pseudomembrane, sometimes covering the inside of the uterus, or ragged, dirty red or red-black in color and gangrenous. Septic endometritis. Septic infection of the uterine wall or abdominal viscera. Severe anemia. Skin eruptions. *Staphylococcus aureus*. Streptococci septicemia. Stupor. Suffocation. Suppurative endometritis. Suppurative phlebitis. Sweats. Tetanus. Uterine necrosis (with gas bubble formation). Vegetative endocarditis. Vomiting. Yellowish pus, pus-filled clots in the ovarian and uterine veins.

The Farmacia

 It made me remember the first year or two of menstruation — a time I'd almost forgotten. Still dismayed with feeling the blood and smelling its warm, secret scent on the napkins, just starting with tampons, and my mother not knowing I was using them (I won't allow it, she'd said — they'll ruin your virginity!). Sneaking to the drugstore to buy them anyway. Scuttling up the aisle and laying the little box on the counter by the cash register (with the side that said TAMPAX face down). Looking at the clerk, or at the pharmacist — both men. But not looking, really. Instead, making furtive contact by means of vectors leading from my downcast eyes, to the counter, then bouncing from the counter to his image on the periphery. Feeling flushed, oily, shamed.

So at this farmacia in Juarez, with that cheery, hotel-for-nationals-in-the-Yucatán, white-tiled, medicinal smell and cleanliness... two *auxiliares*, or clerks, were standing behind the counter, clad in little blue lab coats, looking relaxed and easy without seeming lazy. As I waited for one to wait on me, I gazed at athlete's foot medicine in long narrow boxes, at shallow, elegant blue cups of Nivea creme... feeling more casual than I usually did during this assignment, on which I was investigating the dumping of FDA-banned drugs into Mexico by European and U.S. firms, and for which I had to go around observing the business of Mexican pharmacies and challenging the employees: "Why do you sell prescription medicines without prescriptions?"

As I stood there, one *auxiliar* went into a room behind the counter. There were people in there; I couldn't see them, but the voices sounded like a mother and her small child. "He won't eat and won't take his medicine," she said, and the kid started whimpering desperately: "*¡No! ¡No! ¡No quiero, mami! ¡No quiero!*" Then I heard screams, and realized the auxiliar was injecting the child....

The other auxiliar finally came up, and after I explained my mission, he chatted with me in a most accommodating way. "Oh sure," he shrugged, "we sell everything here. Most of it without prescription. Training? Are you kidding? You get your training by buying a diploma. Doctors, too, of course." Snicker. Wink.

But he was a professional, in his own way — after all, he'd been a *farmacia auxiliar* for 17 years.

The phone rang and he stayed on for a while. It was another *auxiliar*, one who worked a different shift, and they were talking about going fishing in downstate Chihuahua during Easter week when the boss let everyone off for vacation. He hung up and I wanted to keep him talking, so I continued with fish. We'd gotten up to carp when the two girls walked in.

They both had beautiful skin — plump, teenage skin — their eyelids striped with peacock-blue shadow, cheeks silky, arms plump and veinless, waists tummying out in the naked space between their high-cut blouses and slacks. They squiggled and blushed and looked down and mumbled something to the *auxiliar*. He trotted off to the room on the other side of the wall. My senses pricked up; I could hardly wait for him to return so I could see what he'd be bringing back.

He knew I was dying to know.

He tore out of the back room, two little boxes in hand. Then, magician-like, he gesticulated with half his body and with his whole face; and with a loud, smiling remark, he diverted my gaze away from his hands. Meanwhile, he scooted the boxes down the counter, and the second *auxiliar*, with the lightening smooth moves of a skilled secretary taking shorthand, wrapped the products in brown paper. I almost missed seeing what they were, but not quite.

Birth control pills.

At least I think they were. All I saw with certainty were the tiny, plosive smiles on the faces of the girls, and by the way they walked out the door, bouncing, you could tell this was their absolute favorite farmacia. Then the *auxiliares* took their places behind the counter again, easy and dignified in their little blue coats. We looked straight at each other, talked some more. Bass, perch, trout, bait. And I felt my menarche lurking in the deeps behind the fish.

Sabat's Fifteen Minutes of Fame

Anyone who's spent time in Mexico has seen its handicapped. The poor ones, at least, are impossible to miss — the lame and the halt spend even more time on the streets scrabbling a living than do their "normal" underemployed countrymen. Mexico is teeming with blindmen led by seeing-eye children; harelips with holes in their faces; the legless with their homemade "prostheses" that in this country are better known as wheelbarrows.

And there are the deafmutes. Once, in a little town near Acapulco, I ran across a group of children, and in the center of the circle, the village goatherd. He was a young man, heart-throbbingly handsome, intelligent, and awesomely, chillingly, speechless. He asked me for a cigarette by showing me the "sign language" he'd invented during a life without schooling. For *Alas*, the Mexican brand whose name weans "wings," he flapped his arms. For the *Fiesta* brand, he danced around an invisible sombrero. When he strained to speak, he could utter nothing but grunts and groans. The kids told me he was trying to say he wanted to marry the gringa and go to the United States. Translating this for me, they burst into peals of laughter. The deafmute understood nothing of the fun except that the joke was on him. But he smiled weakly anyway, for clearly he knew that the mockery of children was the most attention he'd ever get.

"Sabat," the mystery boy who made big news in the U.S. awhile back, would have been just another Mexican deafmute had he not

managed to reach the border and invent a sign for the Marlboro
Man. For awhile, the media thought they'd come upon a North
American — or at least a white boy — lost in the wilds of Mexico.
What a scoop! It was supposed to be very romantic.

The real story was far different, but the truth was preceded by
weeks of hype. It all began with El Paso's state child protection agency, the Texas Department of Human Services (DHS). God knows,
DHS needs some favorable media attention — across the state, the
agency was under fire in 1988 for failing to protect children because
of its woefully inadequate funding, professional incompetency, or
both. That spring El Paso DHS had been the subject of State Senate
hearings where County Attorney Joe Lucas described five instances of
DHS neglect, including three children who had died after shoddy
casework failed to remove them from their eventually fatally abusive
homes.

Then there was El Paso DHS involvement in yet another fiasco:
the Noble/Dove daycare sex abuse case [see "The Making of a
Modern Witch Trial" and "Sex, the Devil and Daycare"]. In putting
that case together, DHS social workers had done terribly amateurish,
leading, and suggestive interviewing of tiny kids. The accused teachers were at first convicted, but by spring, 1988, one had been acquitted at retrial. Now, tongues were wagging about how the agency and
its shoddy work might have led to false accusations.

But in the midst of all these problems, DHS had at least one
thing to crow about: it was initiating an innovative, binational effort
to coordinate child protection efforts with its Juarez sister organization, DIF, whose initials stand in Spanish for Integrated Family
Development. The idea was that if DIF got a report on a missing
Mexican kid, Juarez would phone El Paso to alert authorities in case
the child had crossed the international line. Or if a parent abused an
El Paso child while the family was visiting Juarez, DIF would call
north to tell DHS to take action. A great idea — now child protec-
tors on both sides would enjoy the best of each other's know-how.
And, unfortunately, the worst.

DHS and DIF shook hands over their binational agreement, and
a few months later, on a cold November Saturday night, a young
woman named Guadalupe de la Vega was driving in Juarez near the
international bridge. Suddenly she spotted a little boy wandering
around. De la Vega, who heads the Mexican tourism office in El Paso,

comes from a prominent, well-to-do Juarez family. Her mother is internationally famous for running a private birth control agency, and both parents socialize and do business frequently in El Paso and farther north. De la Vega has an American education and speaks excellent English. For people like her, the U.S.-Mexico border is little more than a squiggle on a map or a pesky traffic line at the bridge.

So de la Vega found this kid one night. He was cute and fairskinned and freckled and couldn't talk or hear. He kept pointing towards the airport, but when they got there, no one knew him. De la Vega took the boy to her parents' house and named him "Sabat," an occult variation on the word for Saturday. Sabat stayed with her family three weeks; then she put him in DIF's local orphanage. She used to take him home on weekends, and after awhile she started thinking. Sabat knew how to play electronic games, enjoyed breakdancing, and preferred hamburgers over tacos. De la Vega, who is certainly in a geographic and social position to appreciate Mexico's invasion by transnational junk culture, had apparently developed some kind of amnesia. She certainly had not acquired a copy of *Video Night in Kathmandu*. In any event, she decided Sabat must be a gringo. She and the DIF orphanage people contacted El Paso's DHS and posed the theory. DHS assigned the boy a caseworker.

All of a sudden, the news was full of "Sabat May Be American Survivor of Mexico Plane Crash" headlines. The media, from *People Magazine* and the *National Enquirer* to CNN and "Good Morning America," trekked down to the border, and the world was served copy about Sabat drawing pictures of planes with dead people lying around them that were supposed to represent his parents and sister.

Meanwhile, just in case he was missing but not orphaned, the FBI started tracking down milk-carton leads pouring in from Illinois, Los Angeles, Oklahoma, Canada, London, Australia, even France. The French connection, the most romantic and therefore most heralded, fizzled out after the supposedly missing *garcon* was found playing in his yard in East El Paso. It was back to square one for the Feds.

DHS held a big press conference, and, as the *El Paso Times* later noted, "put Sabat through his paces." The reporter who covered the story told me the little boy was desperately eager to perform and to please his caretakers. She said the DHS shindig disgusted her — caseworkers badgered Sabat to draw plane crash pictures, and it was a DHS worker and de la Vega, not Sabat, who had first drawn such scenes. Another caseworker, who does not know sign language, made a show of gesticulating with Sabat, then she told reporters he was telling her he felt "dizzy" after the plane crash.

Assistant El Paso County Attorney Ken Barnes, who prosecutes juvenile sex offenders, later said DHS personnel had recently sent him an affidavit describing how a three-year-old girl used anatomically correct dolls to describe how a boy had sexually assaulted her. But Barnes saw a videotape of the DHS interview, and he says it was a caseworker who was playing with the dolls, not the child. He was so angry that he sent a complaint to the agency at the regional level. "I wouldn't even trust DHS to report a date accurately," Barnes said. He added that a lot of people around the courthouse were cynical about the Sabat story "as though Mexico and DHS don't have enough street kids in El Paso already that need help."

After awhile, even the local media started catching on to the scam. The *Times* reporter saw Sabat using gestures typical of Mexican kids, not Americans. One doctor noted that he had a TB vaccination, which Americans almost never get. Another pointed out that Sabat knew no formal sign language and had apparently never been to school — which would be almost unheard of for even the poorest U.S. child.

Still, there was this need to use Sabat as some sort of Rorschach inkblot. "What if his parents didn't want anyone to know he existed? What if they hid him? What if his father was an American drug trafficker in Mexico?" Guadalupe de la Vega asked me.

On the day she posed those questions, the *El Paso Times* had already located Sabat's family in Tampico, a Gulf Coast town where the street urchins breakdance, eat MexDonaldburgers, and play video games. Sabat's indigent mother is separated, has four other kids, and works long hours in a bar. She is hard pressed to care for the boy, and he runs away a lot. Last year he hitchhiked a ride to his dad's in Monterrey. From there, he apparently thumbed rides to the border. He wanted to go back to his home, though. It's right next to the Tampico airport.

Now that the true story, in all its humdrum drabness, is out, the hoopla is over. The orphanage put Sabat, whose real name is Chuy, on a Mexican bus and sent him back to Tampico. Chuy chugged off with an American-donated hearing aid, amidst speculation that his poverty-stricken mother might manage to educate him only by giving him up to some rich family — Mexican or American.

So that's the story. But what of the myth? What did those weeks of hype really mean? First, that if everyone had known right off that Sabat was Mexican, you can bet you'd never have heard of him. Mexico's neglect of its poor kids can arguably be explained by the country's economic bankruptcy. But as for the Global Village, it wouldn't have given a damn about Chuy if he hadn't sported those gringo freckles.

Here are some other border kid stories to prove my point:

A few years ago, construction workers demolishing a barbecue restaurant in El Paso found the smoked mummy of a Mexican boy in the chimney. His body had been there for months; authorities determined he'd probably gotten trapped while trying to burglarize the place. The neighbors remembered him as an illegal alien who hung around the area, homeless and available for odd jobs. He looked to be about 14 years old. No one ever took him in or knew his name.

Then there was the recent case of an eight-year-old boy who got lost in Southern Arizona. He and his family had traveled from southern Mexico and crossed the border illegally on foot, intending to walk through the desert until they reached a U.S. city. The child accidentally got separated from the others and wandered for two weeks before he was found dead of exposure. Authorities could not understand why, in an area replete with farms and ranches, he had not approached a house to ask for help. The mystery was solved when a ranchowner reported that many days earlier, she'd seen the child, but found him frightening. So she fired a gun at him. Apparently that was the last time he ever asked for help.

What *can* you do if you're a poor Mexican kid who needs attention? Spin tall tales, perhaps, and hope they hook someone from the other side. In a Juarez colonia, some children swore they'd sighted the Virgin Mary. Others near Chihuahua City declared they were regularly socializing with a small group of creatures from Mars. These stories attracted the interest of the Mexican press; they proved a bit too tasteless for the El Paso media. But Sabat was perfect.

It's not just Mexican minors who cater to Americans. The conservative PAN (National Action Party) is masterful at courting U.S. reporters, editors, and conservative politicos by sending English-speaking, American-suited emissaries over the border and even to Washington to speak at every venue from university forums to right-wing think tank luncheons. Even the ruling party, PRI, is learning how to out-Sabat the PAN: last year it hired an American public relations firm to package presidential candidate Carlos Salinas de Gortari and market him to the American media.

We have our own part in the Sabat myth. For us, the story is more an updating of Tarzan: a rehashing of Imperialism's obsession with "civilized" man's proper role in the "jungle." In the fairy tale of the pre-World War II Empire, Africa is filled with comical, childlike natives while Tarzan is a virile, muscular adult. With Sabat, we've reached the age of revolutionary decolonization. Africa is now Latin America, and with Castro and the Sandinistas running around, Mexico is no longer an entity we and the Rulers are supposed to pat benignly on the head. And what of Tarzan? That big hunk of a white guy has shrunk. Now he's a mere kid — weak, mute, deaf to the geopolitical whisperings going on right in front of him — lost in the Third World.

Won't somebody please find out where he belongs and get him out of here?

— *1988*

Adjustment of Status: The Trial of Margaret Randall

I will not follow language
like a dog with its tail between its legs.

from "Immigration Law,"
a poem by Margaret Randall

One lovely spring week in 1986, El Paso offered itself up for use as a landfill. Not for nuclear wastes, nor for the illegal residues of errant multinational factories. Instead, we accepted what playwright Arthur Miller has called "the garbage left behind by the sinking of the great scow of McCarthyism."

The event was the deportation hearing of New Mexico writer Margaret Randall. Local immigration officials had decided several months earlier that she was grist for the McCarran-Walter Act, which at the time still barred foreigners from this country if they were "ideological undesirables." What was an ideological undesirable? Among other things, an anarchist or a Communist. Or someone who wrote things that sounded Communist. Or who published such stuff, or passed it out on street corners. Or who, even if not actually a member, did things like giving speeches supporting a Communist group.

When McCarran-Walter was passed in 1952, the Cold War was in full chill, and Congress believed Communist Parties worldwide were conspiring to use deceit, treachery and terrorism to conquer the Free World. Despite this paranoia, even President Truman was appalled by McCarran-Walter. "Seldom has a bill exhibited the distrust evidenced here for citizens and aliens alike," he said as he vetoed it, adding that "to punish an undefined 'purpose' is thought control."

His veto overridden, we got the Act anyway. And indeed, in Orwellian fashion, the McCarran-Walter Act strove to protect Americans from "alien" thoughts by insuring that people here wouldn't come in contact with controversial foreigners — and especially, foreigners with left political connections and ideas. No one, no matter how renowned, was immune to the censors at the border: English writer Graham Greene; Spanish filmmaker Luis Buñuel; Canadian naturalist Farley Mowat; Nobel Prize winners Gabriel Garcia Marquez of Colombia and Chilean Pablo Neruda; Mexico's Carlos Fuentes; Czech philosopher Czeslaw Milosz; South African writer Dennis Brutus; Italian playwright Dario Fo; Chilean presidential widow and activist Hortensia Allende; Nicaraguan politician/poet Tomás Borge — all were denied permission to visit and speak in the United States.

They were foreigners whose visas were denied before they ever set foot on U.S. soil, and that meant the government didn't have to prove its claims that they were Communists or dangers to national security. Margaret Randall, though, lives right up Interstate 25, in Albuquerque. She has a New York accent — a native one — and she's always called herself a U.S. citizen. But in 1985, the Immigration and Naturalization Service people in El Paso (the office in charge of affairs in Albuquerque) didn't see it that way. As far as they were concerned, Randall had relinquished her citizenship during the Sixties while in Mexico. And because she then spent years in Cuba and Nicaragua, writing nice things about leftist revolutions and bad things about American domestic and foreign policy, the INS decided she deserved the worst they could mete out: a good, swift, McCarran-Walter-style kick out of the country.

Randall didn't take this decision lying down, and neither did a phalanx of civil liberties attorneys and prominent writers like Alice Walker, Kurt Vonnegut, Toni Morrison and William Styron. They filed a federal lawsuit challenging the constitutionality of the act. Meanwhile, it so happens that if you're already here and the government thinks you shouldn't be, they've got to prove their claims against you. A hearing was thus scheduled in immigration court to rule on whether Randall was a Mexican citizen, and if so, whether she should be deported. The venue was El Paso.

When all this happened, I was working as a general assignments reporter for the *El Paso Times*. The day before the proceedings were to start, the federal beat reporter went on vacation, so I ended up with the Randall assignment. Someone passed by my desk and dropped off briefing material: a xerox of the INS denial of her application for permanent residency, and a lengthy magazine article about the case.

Reading it, I got an unexpected flashback to my adolescence. Houston in the mid-Sixties… humid, suburban, cloying, Civil Rights and the New Left still around the corner, but edgily so. Taking the city bus by myself, to a tobacco and newsstand between Rice University and downtown. The smell of cigars, the sheen of porn magazines splayed on old wood racks. Farther in the back, perusing, in my desperate/callow, still-stuck-at-home-in-Houston-but-smoldering-rebellion way, Siren journals from the East Village, the Haight.

And from Mexico. Once, I remember, I blew some of the money I made from my after-school Luby's coffee-cart-girl job on a little poetry magazine heady with the cheap mimeograph smell of Third World newsprint, published half in English and half in Spanish. The logo was a saxophone or trumpet adorned with quetzal feathers. It was called *El Corno Emplumado/The Plumed Horn*. Randall, it turns out, was co-editor.

She was a bohemian practically by pedigree — born in 1936 in Scarsdale to parents who performed classical music, took the children on long junkets to Spain and the Third World, and moved, when Margaret was ten, from the East Coast to Albuquerque. For newcomers like the Randalls, postwar New Mexico's lure wasn't atom bombs or Los Alamos, but the mystique signified by the D.H. Lawrence-Mabel Dodge Lujan arts scene around Taos and Santa Fe. The family ensconced itself in the literary culture of Hispano-America. Margaret's mother has translated Jose Marti's work from Spanish. Her brother owns Salt of the Earth, a shop near New Mexico University that could pass for any hip bookstore in Berkeley, except for its additional emphasis on Latin American politics, history, and works by locals like Jimmy Santiago Baca. Margaret herself started writing early — her first published article, a travel piece, appeared in the *Christian Science Monitor* when she was thirteen.

So it wasn't surprising that in the late 1950s, after abandoning college drama studies, marrying and divorcing, she would move to New York's Lower East Side and start composing poetry while hanging out with writers and artists like Willem de Kooning. Her politics then were characterized by marches she joined against nuclear testing and the Portuguese fascist dictatorship. She toasted Cuba's revolution back when it was a *cause celebre* among liberals, voted for Kennedy in 1960, and called herself a Democrat. Within Randall's milieu, none of this was unusual. And given her affinity for the Beats, it wasn't odd when, unmarried, she deliberately got pregnant by Black Mountain poet Joel Oppenheimer, then took off for Mexico City with only the baby for company.

There she fell in with a group of poets, including Sergio Mondragon. They soon married, had two children, and began producing *El Corno Emplumado/The Plumed Horn. Corno* came out quarterly and garnered international interest because of the bilingual forum it offered writers from the whole of the Americas. Its English section published the first work in translation of Latin American literary giants like Octavio Paz and Ernesto Cardenal. Simultaneously, Spanish speakers were introduced to poets like Diane Wakowski and Allen Ginsberg. Mondragon did the translating from English to Spanish. Randall went vice versa. She thus saw and published a lot of poetry from Hispanic leftist poets, including Cubans.

And in late 1966, she committed the act that, two decades later, would run her up against McCarran-Walter — she applied for a Mexican passport.

Why did she do it? Long before her hearing in El Paso, she said giving up her U.S. citizenship was involuntary and thus by law invalid, that she did it because Sergio was turning into an Eastern religion freak, spending all his time meditating, not supporting the family, leaving that task to her. She said it was very hard for foreigners to find work in Mexico, that all she could get were irregular gigs like translating comic books. She said giving up her citizenship was an error, a mistake, bad judgment, she wished she hadn't done it.

The U.S. government would later insist, though, that Randall's renunciation was the height of voluntarism — the behavior of a raving anti-American trying to make a political statement.

For whatever reason she did it, right after Randall got her Mexican passport, she made her first visit to Cuba to attend a poetry conference. She returned transfixed, and credited the Cuban revolution with making her feel she'd "died and been reborn." She divorced Mondragon, took over *El Corno*, and increasingly parroted

Third World nationalist rhetoric stylish among the New Left — the Che/Fidel/Huey wall-poster scene put in words. Her politics were reinforced by Robert Cohen. A New Yorker in search of guerrilla war, he headed south in 1968 and got no farther than Mexico City. There he assumed the co-editorship of *El Corno*. He also became Randall's lover.

Cohen was 22 years old when they got together, nine years Randall's junior, and he strutted and suffered from all the power, headiness and foolishness of his age, her age, and the Age. To read Cohen from that period is to wince — his boyish posturing and narcissism is so utterly New Left, and so utterly American, that just about any American who passed through those times — even an INS official — has got to feel a shock of self-recognition.

Take Cohen's introduction to Randall's 1973 collection of poetry and diary entries: *Part of the Solution/Portrait of a Revolutionary* — the book which seemed to especially infuriate the Immigration people. Actually, the bulk of the writing here is not by Cohen, but by Randall, who is the self-proclaimed solution and revolutionary of the book's title. Some of her work is powerful: especially her writing about Mexico. She and Cohen ultimately fled the country to escape reprisals for their involvement in the 1968 student movement that ended in the government massacre at Tlateloco. But while she lived in Mexico, Randall used the middle class radicals and literati she worked with as subjects for several sensitive pieces.

When she writes in one essay, for instance, about the double suicide of two five-year-old girl friends (they jumped from their respective highrise apartment windows), she weaves sociology and eternal mysteries into something at once flinty, angry, melancholy and spooky. After all, Randall *knows* the world of the petit-bourgeoisie — she's part of it, even if she hates it. She is also a fine translator, and the book includes her renderings of work by poets like Leonel Rugama, Carlos Maria Gutierrez and Roque Dalton — most of them activists who died doing politics, but who still managed to pick up their pens between guerrilla battles, defeats, and appointments with the torturer.

When it comes to writing of her own experience with Revolution, though, Randall turns into a hopeless preacher, and worse, a didactic model of the New Socialist Man. The bulk of *Part of the Solution*, for instance, is about Cuba. Or to be specific, about Randall and Cohen in Cuba. About how great it is to be in Cuba. Or that is, to be a great couple like Cohen and Randall in a great country like Cuba. Kind of like if, during the same historical conjuncture, John and Yoko, instead of doing their bed-in in Manhattan, had taken their percales down to Havana and then written a book about it.

Which brings us back to Cohen's introduction — an interminable account of how Margaret became a revolutionary. We learn that, as a teenager, she kept a travel diary in which she wrote that Lima, Peru, is "extremely dirty." To Cohen, this diary is "one of the 'pure products' of the Amerika Margaret has now dedicated her life to destroying." That's good, because Randall, who used to be a "despicable, warped creature," has fortunately since been transformed by "tremendously powerful forces" that have caused her to "develop into a conscious revolutionary fighter...!"

Wow. All this implied psychological bondage and discipline couched in the hot and brawny, yet prim rhetoric of Mao and the Bolsheviks... you read this stuff and whether you want to or not, you start trying to imagine exactly how Margaret and Robert got it on in bed. It's embarrassing to be faced with your own prurience. But you go on reading. You are not entirely disappointed.

For, indeed, we learn from Cohen the minutiae of Randall's problems with her sexuality. She is hung up, for instance, about her small breasts and excess facial hair; and it is understood that we are to blame this on capitalism. In addition, Cohen reviews Margaret's checkered relationships with the men who preceded him. About her first husband, for instance, we learn that he liked to beat her and make her lie perfectly still during sex. This again is in some way correlated with, if not caused by, imperialism and/or commodity fetishism: Cohen reminds us that this first husband, whom he calls "American Sam," abused Margaret in the presence of "all the wonderful electric appliances they got as wedding presents as witnesses."

Cohen wants us to know that for years, while with these men, Randall didn't feel like a "real woman." But "for a person who closes so completely, her openness in love, physically, her abandon, is really amazing." For this he claims modest credit: "It was only at the age of 31, stimulated by a new relationship of relative health and real passion, and strengthened by a new collective consciousness developing with the Women's Liberation movement in the States, that Margaret began to penetrate the terrible armor of role oppression. A *real* woman? Right on!"

(In speaking of his own role oppression, Cohen is also political-ly-correctly humble: When Randall began to "righteously challenge the monster privilege of double standard in me," he writes, "I was struck impotent for two whole months…")

When Randall finally begins her section of *Part of the Solution*, with diary excerpts from their first year in Cuba, her tone is infused with a similar, fevered slavishness. Now we read of a thoroughfare "alive with Lenin, his presence in image and word, and the dictums are particularly apt for the daily struggle in Cuba now: that need for constant heroism in everyday work…." Castro (whom Randall got right up next to during one of his speeches) is breathlessly described as "without doubt the most brilliant, the most courageous, and most humane leader of our or any time." As for her four children, Randall is delighted by "how communist they're becoming!" and she gives an example: when asked why people commit suicide, her ten-year-old son "immediately said it was because of the pressures put on them by a distorted or transitional society, the contradictions people face in their lives provoked by a faulty system which exploits them."

Part of the Solution is so short on the concrete stuff of life that hu-mor (at least, premeditated humor) is virtually absent. But sometimes something funny and vibrant hobbles out. For instance, after the children attend a Cuban livestock show and hear a detailed descrip-tion of animal breeding methods, Randall writes, "Yesterday, on the living room floor, little Annie pulled open Sarah's cunt, and Sarah called in to the kitchen: 'Mommy, Annie's inseminating me!'"

Amusing? Probably not to El Paso INS director A. H. Giugni, who made the original decision to go after Randall. Giugni's deporta-tion order avoids quoting *Part of the Solution's* sexual passages, con-centrating instead on the damning "political" evidence of her unde-sirability ("Ms. Randall," he notes, "makes reference to the badge of the law enforcement officials as a 'coward's shield' … and writes 'monster Amerikkka in the pit of her blackest cesspool gut…'"). But Randall has written thousands of pages of other work to choose from, and the odd thing is that more than half of what Giugni quotes to show her "undesirability" comes from that one book. It seems that of everything Randall produced, the government was most obsessively offended by this rather innocuous if overeager collaboration between a New Left woman and her young lover.

Al Giugni is an odd, sad-looking man. It's not just his note-worthy obesity and trembling, down-hanging jowls. It's more the jarring combination of his massive poundage versus his tiny Oriental features. Giugni is part Hawaiian, which gives him a rather Samoan look. Samoan with a touch of Mediterranean — er-go his Italian surname.

Despite Giugni's less-than-precise appearance, he has a crisp, almost close-mouthed way of talking. It's one well suited to quoting six-digit figures interspersed with decimals, parentheses, lower-case letters, and words like "section," "subsection," "alienage" and "equities" — the dispassionate numerology and argot of the federal immigration statutes.

In keeping with his job, Giugni seems Government-issue and colorless. But he has been known to display occasional flairs for the dramatic. For instance, in 1986, he set up the INS's first-ever sting operation. It seems the agency was having trouble rounding up a bunch of illegal alien El Pasoans who refused to answer their door-bells — they had long ago been caught, given deportation hearings and ordered out of the country. So Giugni mailed them phony invita-tions to a raffle where they were guaranteed to win a diamond neck-lace or a Ford Bronco XLT. Excited moms and dads flocked to the "contest" with their kids, and the INS agents met them dressed as clowns, and even handed out balloons and popcorn. Then they herded the families into an armory, put the adults in vans and deported them.

As INS directors go, though, Giugni's got a reputation for being humanitarian. If an undocumented Mexican is sick and needs treat-ment in the U.S., Guigni will cut the red tape and wave the poor soul through. He can do things like that because immigration rules are civil, not criminal law, so the district director has a lot of leeway in deciding who gets in and who doesn't.

That leeway is called "discretion," and when it comes to the INS, discretion is the name of the game. Basically, it means that if you want something from them, don't yell, don't sneer, don't go to the press, don't demand your rights, don't criticize, don't quote statu-tory law. Just smile, ask, beg, be polite, be nice! Doesn't matter who you are: immigrant, lawyer, reporter — or radical poet.

Discretion was not Margaret Randall's forte. Not only did she live in Cuba, she was an outspoken supporter of the revolution there, touted the progress of women in socialist countries like Viet Nam, and denounced U.S. racism and imperialism in books, poems and speeches. When talking to the U.S. press, she was cheeky about her Leninism, too — in Havana in 1977, for instance, she told a Washington Post journalist, "What is that terrible phrase in the bourgeois language, 'I disapprove of what you say but I will defend to the death your right to say it.' Well, I hate that. One has values in life and they are what they are."

But as time passed, her writing got more mellow and sometimes more resonant, especially when she began doing oral histories with radical women in socialist countries. Randall has a good ear for dialogue, and when she lets her subjects speak they come off earthy and eloquent. On the other hand, when she tries to put what these women are personally experiencing into broader perspective, she's about as exciting as a footnote in an annual government report — as in her endless listings of Cuban health statistics: "each local polyclinic served 9,000... over 9,000 pediatric beds...with a variance of from 0.9 to 1.2 among the provinces... Pregnancies averaged in obstetrical visits each, with a variance of 7.6 and 10.3 among the different provinces...."

In 1980, Randall, who had long since split up with Cohen, moved to Nicaragua to work for a women's group and advise the government on how to banish sexism and racism from the media. But Nicaragua was in the midst of a U.S.-sponsored civil war, and the violence plaguing the country began to wear Randall out. She finally suffered a nervous breakdown of sorts, and a therapist recommended she leave Nicaragua to get a rest. Too, Randall's father was ill, and she wanted to be with her parents in Albuquerque, where she could relax, do photography, write, and, as she put it later, spend time "seeking solutions to problems, in dreams." She came back to the U.S. on a visitor's visa in early 1984, married an old friend, poet Floyce Alexander, and got a job teaching American and Women's Studies at the University of New Mexico. She also petitioned the INS for permanent residency.

Returning to the Southwest wasn't just nostalgic, it was also replete with America, which nowadays, for a radical, is not so much Amerikkka as Ameriggga — i.e., morally muddied, politically slogged down, boring, demoralized, televised and ultra-commoditized.

Randall kept a diary (later published as *Albuquerque: Coming back to the U.S.A.*) in which she did a lot of kvetching. She complained that when Americans send xeroxed Christmas letters, they mention not a word about Central America, South Africa, Chicago's West Side or Afghanistan. She was obsessed about her eating binges (chocolate sundaes), worried about excess facial hair, watched the movie *Clockwork Orange* and the band Kiss on TV and clucked over their cynicism like a proletkult schoolmarm. Even when she went bowling with her nephew, she didn't just have fun; she had to assure her diary that it is good to enjoy oneself while bowling and correct to have fun.

Things seemed to be going at that leisurely if neurotic pace most middle class sunbelters enjoy now that we've transferred our break-neck assembly lines, subhuman wage levels and armed conflicts to places like the one Randall had just left. But then life got much more problematic. An INS agent read Randall's permanent residency application, noticed where she'd been living the past two decades, grilled her about her politics and sent her papers down to El Paso for Al Giugni's perusal.

A year later, Giugni did something perhaps even more dramatic than his sting operation: he denied Randall her green card — and not by referring to statutes, but simply on grounds of discretion. That means that, instead of invoking a law to keep Randall out, Giugni simply decided he personally didn't want her here. Why? Because Randall's "writings go far beyond mere dissent, disagreement with, or criticism of the United States." Giugni didn't say she was a threat to our security, or to anything or anyone else, for that matter. He simply thought Randall's ideas were "detrimental to the national interest." So he set himself up as the feds' official border censor and ordered her to quit the country. Randall refused to go without a fight, and the hearing was set.

From the beginning, it was a scene. Giugni was nowhere in sight — now that the issue had gone to court, the government was invoking statutes claiming Randall was more than just someone the district director wasn't fond of. Now, as per McCarran-Walter, she stood accused of being an affiliate, or even a member, of the Communist Party. Not only that, the government said, she advocated totalitarianism, the killing of cops, *and* she was "against the happiness and good order of the United States."

The government's arguments on these points were to be made by
INS attorneys Guadalupe Gonzalez and Penny Smith. Both dressed
in cheap suits that made them look like down-at-the-heels airline
stewardesses. Gonzalez was scrubbed and eager looking, whereas
Smith had a disconcertingly empty face, rather like a Barbie Doll, or
one of Hugh Hefner's wives. Randall's defense would be handled by
attorney Michael Maggio, an erstwhile student radical, cum National
Lawyers Guild attorney, who had already litigated against McCarran-
Walter restrictions in several previous cases. Joining Maggio were
Michael Ratner and David Cole of the Center for Constitutional
Rights, a New York-based law office founded by people like William
Kunstler. All of them had a politically progressive amount of hair on
their heads, and/or appropriately rumpled suits.

On the other hand, the male lawyers for the INS, who were
hanging around the courtroom waiting for the show, were closely
cropped and haberdashed, and the rest of the government audience
consisted of INS secretaries — Hispanic women sporting high heels,
lavish eyeshadow and mascara, and bright, flowery dresses. Randall's
supporters, many of whom were her students, were another story —
one El Paso is seldom exposed to. They were vintage Santa
Fe/Albuquerque feminists: women, mostly Anglo, with no-nonsense
haircuts, parsimonious makeup, earth shoes, tee-shirted pregnancies
and long Guatemalan skirts. In just about any other place, it would
have been charming to see these two kinds of people together. But
this was a courtroom, and one group was calling the other undesirable. It was not a happy affair.

The hearing was to be divided into two sections. The second
part would deal with whether Randall was a commie. But those arguments might not ever take place — not if her lawyers could successfully argue during the first day that she never voluntarily renounced
her U.S. citizenship. Was Randall actually still an American? If so,
her political expressions were protected, and the final, deportation
part of the proceeding would be canceled.

She took the stand clutching a bottle of nose drops.

Randall was a short, overweight woman, almost 50 years old,
with long, gray hair held back in a clip, wearing a loose peasant dress
sewn from textiles that looked handwoven and Central American.
You could tell this was her Sunday-go-to-meeting look, and it was
reasonable to imagine her bumping around in Albuquerque looking

even more gravely casual, probably with her hair free and billowing. Altogether, she had that black and white, crystalline look you see in the book jacket photos of aging women novelists and poets.

But it soon became obvious that as much as anything else, Randall's dignity was on trial here. Her attorneys were dealing very seriously with the renunciation of citizenship issue — they wanted to make a strong argument that Randall had given it up solely because of economic hardship and ignorance of the consequences.

This meant she had to stress her poverty and problems in Mexico, and she made some points that anyone would consider sensible — the fact, for instance, that her infant daughter had been seriously ill. And in need of expensive medical treatment. On the other hand, many of the courtroom colloquies about Randall's hard times came off sounding ridiculous, especially to *fronterizos*, who have lived in relative intimacy with Mexican misery on both sides of the border. There was the exchange when Randall described how she'd been so poor, she'd had to sell pozole (a hominy stew) in front of her house, and "in Mexico, *pozolera*" — a woman who sells the stew — "is slang for woman of ill repute. My husband wouldn't speak to me for months." To this the government countered that she'd had a maid; but Randall's lawyers, brandishing an affidavit from an anthropologist, explained that even poor Mexicans employ servants. Amid all this, the Albuquerque feminists clucked, the Juarez Trotskyists sitting next to me chortled, the INS lawyer bystanders sneered, and the secretaries shook their heads — all with their separate disbeliefs.

But then things got downright vicious as government attorney Guadalupe Gonzalez began casting crude, catty aspersions on Randall's morals while ostensibly trying to demonstrate that she'd always had an erratic employment history. As Randall sat graying and asthmatic in her witness chair, the thirtysomethingish Gonzalez wheeled around like Perry Mason, demanding to know if Randall had "worked in a gay bar in New York City in the 1950s?"

And how about as a nude model?

"As an artist's model," answered Randall.

"And in the nude?" insisted Gonzalez.

"And clothed," Randall explained stoically.

Gonzalez also kept implying that Randall had given up her citizenship to make a political statement. On the face of it, this has always seemed preposterous to me, for three reasons. For Randall is a person who does *nothing* without rushing for a piece of paper to write about how great it was how she did it and that everyone else should do it too. And yet, even during her Right On days, those years when she replaced her "c's" with the letter "k," Randall never wrote a word about renouncing her citizenship. Second, I cannot imagine why any foreign leftist today, even one out to make a political splash, would trade U.S. citizenship for a Mexican passport. Mexico, after all, has a notorious rep among radicals for being the most deformed, perverted socialist state in history — it's almost completely under the aegis of transnational capital and policy; and the income disparity between its lower and upper classes is more glaring and cruel than in any other country. I'm sure Randall knew all this; after all, she lived there.

And third, the Cold War may have obfuscated and hypocritized Americans' true, hardnosed habits when it comes to citizenship. But here on the border, the real story is right under our noses. One of El Paso's most celebrated founding fathers, for instance, Kentucky-born James Magoffin, came to the El Paso area in the 1830's, when it was still Mexican property. He then promptly set out to get rich by brokering merchandise from Missouri to Chihuahua. Like Randall did 150 years later, he also promptly took a Mexican spouse; such arrangements were said to be good for business. And Magoffin traded in his native citizenship, also a common practice among his *gringo* peers. He never gave much indication that he felt allegiance to Mexico — even while a citizen of that country, he moved his operations and family to Missouri; and during the U.S.-Mexico War, he aided and abetted the U.S. Army. But no matter. Today, Magoffin's palatial mansion is a state park, a street is named for his family, and no one gives a damn that he pulled a Margaret Randall.

And Randall probably wouldn't have upset many people either if the INS had concentrated on her Magoffinism. After all, the supreme rationale for doing almost anything these days is that you're just taking care of business. That's why the government lawyers ignored the hohummery of the cash nexus and emphasized the far more charged issue of Randall's leftism.

"Is it true that story I've heard about you fixing a *paella* for Fidel Castro when he was in New York?" Gonzalez asked. "The paella was never delivered," corrected Randall. And sometimes, Gonzalez mixed up the most potent slur of all, politics and sex:

"Did you smuggle diaphragms into Spain?"

"That's stretching things a bit."

"Is it true you danced in a cabaret?"

"I danced flamenco," Randall sighed.

Then, getting really nasty, Gonzalez, paraphrasing the hated *Part of the Solution*, asked Randall, "Who do you consider the most courageous, brilliant, outstanding leader of this time or any time?" "Objection!!" yelled her lawyer. "Unless you're going to ask her favorite food or TV show!"

All these demurrals and explanations and objections by Randall seemed profoundly sad to me — and chilling. Here was a woman, old enough to be a grandmother, who'd obviously lived a decent and passionate life; with an excellent mind, ear and pen for some things, a poor one for others. She'd done and written some very smart things. And some really stupid ones, too. Just like most everyone else. And yet, here she was on trial about her life, and she couldn't even stand up and say "Fuck You, Uncle Sam, and Fuck You, INS! I posed naked and danced all night, I sneaked birth control through Bilbao and had wet dreams about Fidel. I dig revolution and what socialism does for women's health, and for children, and for poetry, and yes, we're often fools. And if you don't like it, Up Yours — I'm here and I'm staying!"

But she didn't do this. She was trying to be "reasonable," "responsible," "discreet." *Contrite*. But with all this, the judge still ended the U.S. citizenship half of the hearing by ruling that Randall had given hers up voluntarily. And so the four-day deportation proceeding began.

As the days passed, Randall sat quietly and had to do even more penance and catechism: answering silly rhetorical questions posed not just by the government, but by her lawyers as well. ("Have you ever in your life *not* been attached to the Constitution?" "No. Forcefully, no." "Should we have a Dictatorship of the Proletariat here?" "Not today, no." "Would you like the United States to be happy?" "I would like everyone in this country to be happy and for the people of the world to be happy." But her continued compliance and good manners failed to mollify the INS lawyers — clearly, they despised Randall to the point of foolishness. When Gonzalez and Smith attempted to introduce piles of Randall's Spanish-language essays and poems into the record, for instance, she and her attorneys objected to the terrible quality of the English translations. They had been done not by a professional, but by a chicana bridge tender — one of those civil servants who collects your toll when you drive to Juarez. The translations were illiterate. In one, an essay where Randall described an experience in Cuba, she talked about a literary affair she attended, the "Ruben Darío Conference." The Spanish word for "conference" is the same as for when you meet someone, and the bridge tender had described Randall "meeting" Ruben Darío, a long-deceased poet of the 19th century. Randall agreed with attorney Penny Smith that, by nature, a translation can never come out completely literal. "But it can't say you've met with a person who's been *dead* a hundred years," she protested. To which Smith replied in a soft, seance-y voice: "I've read of encounters where people have met with ghosts who've been dead for *two thousand* years. Perhaps you were having one of those."

The week wore on and gradually tempered the shock of being at this strange inquisition. Occasionally, something really interesting would occur — as when poet Adrienne Rich limped into court, arthritic and noble, to offer expert testimony about how Randall's "cesspool gut" and "Amerikka" language was no big thing in the context of the late Sixties; and how no one person, not even Al Giugni, can make the definitive interpretation of what a poem or any other piece of writing "really" means. This was a discussion about the nature of Metaphor, it was being conducted by one of this country's most renowned and brilliant poets, and it was happening in El Paso, Texas — a place I heard a Houston reporter bitching about later that day because it's "so out of the way and the restaurants are terrible and the hotels don't have jacuzzis." Also later that day, I drove Rich down to the Rio Grande; she wanted to talk to the women crossing illegally to work as house maids. We were walking to the embankment very slowly and laboriously — Rich uses a cane — when a green van screeched up. A Border Patrolman climbed out and gave us a good once over. "What are you doing here, girls?" he said.

We answered very politely.

The courtroom, meanwhile, was coming to resemble an upper division political science seminar. After all, the government was alleging that Randall was affiliated with the Communist Party, so it had to prove that the organizations she'd worked for in Cuba and Nicaragua were in fact party organs. In response, her lawyers brought in academic specialists on those countries. One of them, University of New Mexico professor Nelson Valdes, was a Cuban émigrè version of Humphrey Bogart.

In a word, Valdes was cool — unruffled by Gonzalez' and Smith's snipings, and witty in that way one imagines Eastern European samizdat editors to be during their meetings with the censor. The government, for instance, was making much of the fact that Randall had joined the *Federación de Mujeres Cubanas*, worked for the publishing house *Casa de las Américas* and been active in her neighborhood CDR (*Comité por la Defensa de la Revolución*). Valdes pointed out that most Cuban women were members of the *Federación*, and that its main functions were, for example, to provide chaperones for girls going to the country to pick tomatoes "to make sure they don't get in trouble." As for Casa, he noted that it is in the habit of applying for Ford Foundation grants to record U.S. folk music, and that it recently honored a work of New Mexico fiction titled *Tunomás Honey* published by Bilingual Press. And what about the CDR? It organized people to make sure their neighbors didn't play radios too loud. "Guard duty means someone gets a table, you all start playing *dominos*, and hope no one breaks into someone's house," Valdes shrugged gamely.

His insouciant matter-of-factness rankled Smith. "Are you a Marxist?" she demanded. "There are more types of Marxists than Baskin-Robbins ice cream," Valdes retorted. "Do you express sympathy for communists?" she persisted. "You mean if they're dying?"

"Was *Casa de las Américas* political?" "Yes, in the same fashion a marriage often is."

Compared to the INS lawyers' scarcely concealed animus for Randall and her friends, presiding judge Martin Spiegel's bureaucratic disinterest seemed downright friendly. At the start of the proceedings, Spiegel took pains to explain that his role would not be to judge Randall's politics nor the justice or injustice of McCarran-Walter, but simply to rule on whether its edicts about advocating totalitarianism or affiliating with Parties applied to her. He thus treated the writer and her entourage with unfailing civility, and even made his own objections to the government's most ludicrous questions. Gonzalez, for instance, once asked Randall if she was "against private property," and when Speigel objected, Gonzalez protested that she wanted to show that Randall was "not attached to the Constitution." "I don't think it's relevant that a person believes in the right to hold property in this country," countered the judge. "But the Constitution *guarantees* the right to hold property!" said Gonzalez. "The Constitution can be changed," Spiegel explained. "Do you subscribe to the principle that change in government sometimes must be effected by other than peaceful means?" Gonzalez asked Randall. "Objection!" the judge interrupted. "The Constitution permits the right to armed revolution!"

With that, both sides made their closing arguments.

Gonzalez: "Margaret Randall has utter disdain for capitalism...In these time when subversive forces are seeking to infiltrate...she made her application for resident status in the wrong country. The United States is not a hotel!"

Randall's attorney Maggio: "History will show who are the real subversives in this room!"

Judge Spiegel then spent the rest of the spring and summer reading everything Randall had written — almost 3,000 pages worth. And when he closed the last book he made his decision. Randall, he said, was a fine, upstanding contributor to American culture, with lots of U.S. citizen kin to sponsor her green card. There was no proof she'd been a Party member, he concluded, and he never even implied she was any threat to national security. But sorry — Randall's writings, the judge decided, "advocate the economic, international and governmental doctrines of world communism." Her pen had rendered her deportable.

The irony of it all was that, even as Spiegel made his ruling, Cold War shibboleths about international Communist totalitarian conspiracies were subliming into the thaw of Glasnost. And when Guadalupe Gonzalez reargued the government's position at an appeal hearing the next year in Washington, she didn't even pretend Randall posed a national security problem. Now the evil the writer was said to be encouraging was national "ambivalence." Quoting Allen Bloom and *The Closing of the American Mind*, Gonzalez claimed that if we let Randall live here, we might "dilute the battle between freedom and communism to the level of no fault auto insurance...But there *is* a right and wrong. The American Congress has stated that our system of government is right, and it is good, and the communist system is bad...the American door does not swing open to all types of lifestyles, and to all types of political ideologies...We are protecting the national perspective...in favor of God and country, a perspective in favor of freedom and one for which we should never apologize."

Randall's lawyer, David Cole, later summed up Gonzalez' argument: it was a remarkably honest defense of censorship, he wrote, a worldview in which ideas themselves are dangerous. To Cole, the drive to deport Randall was an attempt to celebrate democracy and freedom. But in its desperate yearning for the security blanket of immediate, objective and literal "truth," the effort negated one of democracy's most fundamental rights — free speech.

And if the nation is threatened by writing — writing which means nothing without the myriad renderings of different minds attached to the eyes fixed on pages — then who or what should be deported? The author? The text?

Or the reader?

Randall's appeal dragged on through 1988, even as Congress scrapped McCarran-Walter's ideological exclusion provisions against visiting foreigners (unlike Randall, who was trying to *live* here). Finally, in late 1989, three years after her El Paso hearing, the Board of Immigration Appeals ruled that Judge Spiegel had come down wrong on the citizenship question: Randall hadn't renounced it of her own free will. That meant she'd never lost it.

The government thus mooted all the larger, controversial questions this case entailed. If they weren't resolved, at least Randall's personal fate was. She is still in Albuquerque, still traveling the country teaching and speaking. And though her writing continues to be quieter than it was a generation ago, it remains just as personal, and sometimes just as nasty when referring to the powers that be (a recent poem, for instance, compares El Paso INS officials Al Giugni and Guadalupe Gonzalez to child molesters).

I got a call from Randall one day, several months after the first hearing was over and the appeals still pending. Back at that first proceeding, I had been so revolted by what was being done to this woman that I couldn't help violating Gannett canons of journalistic "objectivity" — I had removed the blue bead necklace I was wearing and given it to her. Later I'd written an op-ed piece expressing my disgust with the whole affair. So Randall considered me her friend — her only friend in these parts, she said. When she called, her daughter Sarah, who came to adulthood in Cuba, was traveling from Havana via Mexico City to visit her mother in Albuquerque. But she'd gotten stranded en route at the Trailways station in El Paso, down the street from me. Would I pick her up?

She was 21 or 22, slender, with long blondish hair, tawny skin and big, doe-eyes — she looked much like what her mother must have at the same age. It was a hot summer night and we poured rum at the kitchen table. She spoke no English. And somehow — it was funny because it didn't happen for any special reason — Sarah started talking about the same things her mom had written about in that book I mentioned before: *Women in Cuba: Twenty Years Later*. Those endless health department statistics about clinic populations and numbers of beds and variance decimals. But when Sarah said it all in her Spanish with no "s's," it wasn't didactic, wasn't a lecture. It was just casual, comfortable talk, from a young woman — spoken in passing, the way a girl at a *quinceañera* declares her virginity for Christ, and you know she'll give it up to her boyfriend soon anyhow, and will still be a perfectly good Catholic. Sarah was utterly charming.

We drove back downtown to catch her bus, parked the car and walked across the darkened street. We were six blocks from Mexico. A Border Patrol van passed and the drivers slowed, appraising Margaret Randall's Cuban, Communist daughter. Then they whistled. First a soft, low whistle, then a high one. Smacking of lips. They took their hands and gesticulated — *Vente!* they said. *Come here!*

Sarah, vaguely amused, smiled and kept walking, without breaking her stride. She was on her way to Albuquerque, and soon she'd be seeing her mother.

Frontier Violence

When out-of-towners first hear the name, they often confuse it with the famous clock in London. That's ironic, since in travel agents' eyes at least, nothing could be farther from England's civilized graces than the Big Bend.

Located on the West Texas-Mexico border hundreds of miles from just about anything, Big Bend National Park is 700,000 acres of arid, mountainous, cactus-strewn, practically people-less topography that got its name because it's surrounded on three sides by the great southward swing of the Rio Grande River.

The *Texas Almanac* says there is no place in the world like the Big Bend. This is no overstatement, since the place looks *extra* terrestrial, with its shockingly sharp, weirdly bleached mountains and desert plants that look less like earthly flora than sci-fi creatures from outer space. On the other hand, the Big Bend's cruel starkness is forgiven in other parts by high-desert streams and greenery, and by canyons cut deep by the cool, swimmable Rio Grande. All in all, the *Almanac* claims, the Big Bend is a world "sculpted by nature, unaltered in any significant way by man."

But once, back when the park's worst dangers still came from nature — from cactus thorns, heat stroke and wild boar attacks — I chanced on its man-made threat: an ecology of commerce and culture that later overwhelmed a river rafter and sniped him to death.

If I'd been a good tourist or even a motorist when I made my first trip to the Big Bend, I probably never would have noticed anything social about the park. But that summer, back in the late '70s, I got there by hitchhiking. A new boyfriend went with me; we'd fallen in love and had a notion that in the stark Chihuahua Desert we'd fall even farther. My car was in the shop, which made it unfit for driving, much less for packing with outback survival gear like food. But what the hell! We were so wrapped up in each other that not until we stuck our thumbs out on I-10 did I look down at my plastic shower zorries and realize I'd forgotten shoes. The boyfriend, a serious bird-watcher, feigned anger — now how were we going to hike to the Big Bend's Boot Springs, the only American habitat of the Colima Warbler? But that was just boyfriend scolding — the only nature we really wanted to explore was each other's. As for the rest, we figured that once we hit the park, society would care for us.

The boyfriend and I eventually got married, and I now remember little about fresh passion and less of Big Bend landscape. What both of us still recall vividly is people — people flowing quietly through all that nature, like giant bacteria, infecting the Big Bend with a fevered morbidity, using the area's divine remoteness as a medium to conduct the age-old business of the border. That business being pilfering, poaching, and smuggling.

One of the first rides we got inside the park was in a late-model pickup driven by a Houston couple. The husband looked like a prosperous retiree and the wife could have sung with the Sweet Adelines. After we exchanged pleasantries, the senior citizens chortled with delight as they pointed out the piles of rocks and cacti they were sneaking off federal land and back to Houston, to implant in their own front lawn. Later we got a hitch with an intense, long-haired young couple in a beat-up car who made their living by driving around at night abducting exotic snakes, sneaking them out of the park, then selling them to pet shops all over the country. The woman sat in the front seat with veiled eyes, the driver bragged how he could see in pitch dark, and we bounced around in the back with a cage of writhing serpents.

Then there were the two strapping blond guys from Odessa. We were on our way from the mountains to the Cottonwoods campground, near Santa Elena, the Mexican pueblo just across the Rio Grande and near the canyon with the same name. The blond guys were real friendly. They said they were going over to Santa Elena "to have a couple beers and talk with the Messkins." It was impossible to imagine why people who used such a word would wish to socialize with its referents. As for us, we needed supper and thought we could find a Santa Elena cafe or housewife willing to cook some beans and rice. When I said we'd like to cross the river too, the blond guys suddenly weren't so hospitable. They dropped us off a ways from the landing; when we arrived there on foot, they'd already caught the "ferry" — a scruffy aluminum canoe. We took it next time around, and on reaching the bluffs of the pueblo, found the Odessans in the middle of a heroin deal.

In a way, it was a casual business. Loose knots of teenaged Mexican boys slouched around in broad daylight fingering their bulging pockets and circling us, asking if we'd like to buy some pot...or anything else? It wasn't much different from the "coke? smoke?" fellows in New York's Washington Square or on the fringes of Harlem; yet there was something more sinister about this scene in this particular place. It was, after all, not just a blip in the variegated life of a city. Dusty little Santa Elena was nothing but a starkly isolated clutch of adobe *jacales*, some goats, loose cattle, old men, women, and boys. And the boys — the pushers — seemed frighteningly bored. I remember watching the happy Odessa blondes depart with their stash, and the dealers outlined in a flaming sunset, crouched silent on a bluff overlooking the endless Hudson-River-School-cum-Martian vista of the Big Bend. My skin crawled, and I remember thinking, in the midst of so much beauty, that I wouldn't want to pass those bluffs on a tourist raft.

Twelve years later, an Eastland, Texas, couple named Heffley were among some 5,000 people who annually float the Rio Grande through its dazzling canyons and rapids. For the Heffleys, though, the trip turned into a nightmare when snipers wounded the wife and a guide, and killed the husband. Two weeks later, four Mexican youths from abject little towns on both sides of the river gave authorities statements indicating that they shot the rafters strictly for the hell of it.

The Mexican media was too abashed by its government censors to say much of anything, and U.S. journalism confined itself to vague sketches of the local drug trade and to detailed handwringing about this bizarre turn of events in what Big Bend area tour operators tout as America's "last unspoiled frontier."

But, as Alan Weisman demonstrates superbly in his book *La Frontera*, (Harcourt, Brace & Jovanovich, 1986), those last two words

— *unspoiled* and *frontier* — are contradictions in terms. *Frontier* means border; and the history of the line where America and Mexico meet is rife not only with wonder, but with spoilation. Weisman and photographer/coauthor Jay Dusard spent a year prowling the 2,000-mile length of the U.S.-Mexico line; and in the sparsely populated Big Bend area, as in teeming Brownsville/Matamoros, El Paso/Juarez, Nogales/Nogales, and San Diego/Tijuana, they saw variations of the modern crisis spawned by 150 years of inequality between First and Third World — a skewing that has long stocked the border with cheap labor, bootleg liquor, and sex for hire. With Mexico's contemporary debt crisis and the arrival of foreign Big Business of all stripes, the inventory now includes displaced peasants, runaway currency, dumped pharmaceuticals, dirty rivers, poisoned air. And most recently, lots of dope — with the typical effects drugs have on a culture, no matter how close to the Sierra Club it may be or how remote from Austin, Washington, Mexico City, and Ciudad Chihuahua.

When Weisman crossed from the Big Bend National Park to Mexico's adjoining Sierra del Carmen mountains, he found the sierra denuded by lumber cutters and local Mexican ecologists helpless to halt the destruction, since their country can ill afford a national park in the middle of nowhere. No park means no guide and tourist concession work for Mexicans, so bread-winners in pueblos like Santa Elena have only a few job possibilities.

Like the tourists do, they can poach animals or cactus. Or *candelilla*, a waxy desert plant that has long been a smuggling mainstay. In America, the Wrigley's company uses candelilla for its chewing gum and Merle Norman likes it for cosmetics. But the vast quantities of stoopback labor required to harvest the plant are more cheaply bought with Mexico's minimum wage, which is only a tenth that in the U.S. So hustlers smuggle Mexican candelilla, export tax unpaid, across the Rio Grande, and take it to Lajitas, Texas. There, a family named Ivey buys tons of it monthly — according to what they themselves told Weisman — and they clear it through the sanguine U.S. Customs office in Presidio before shipping it to a rendering plant in Alpine.

Besides working the candelilla, Mexicans can make a living by working in the United States illegally — a fairly simple effort since the Border Patrol hardly bothers with labor enforcement on America's "last unspoiled frontier." This laxity works out well in

Lajitas, the town where the park ends. There, a rich Houstonian named Walter Mischer is building an "authentic" shoot-'em-out wild west town for filmmakers and tourists. A nearby ghost town, Terlingua, hosts an annual Chili Cook-Off that attracts mobs of tourists. It is surrounded by chunks of desert snapped up by realtor speculators anticipating a resort boom. Terlingua itself is the personal property of the Iveys, the ones who buy the candelilla in Lajitas.

But what if you don't care to pick wax plants, kidnap snakes, or build an ersatz OK Corral? Lately, you can deal drugs.

That's what Pablo Acosta chose. Until recently the state of Chihuahua's biggest *narcotraficante*, Acosta was born in Santa Elena, but as a child left with his destitute family to follow cotton harvests in the U.S. Furiously sucking a joint during an interview in an adoring Mexican policeman's office, Acosta told Weisman how he noticed, while working as an illegal alien in construction in Odessa 20 years ago, that a lot of Americans wanted the heroin coming out of the Big Bend. So Acosta eschewed candelilla and began running smack. He was soon arrested at a roadblock near Marfa and subsequently served five years in Fort Leavenworth. When he got out, he built a thriving drug business by plugging into Mexico's Pancho Villa/Robin Hood tradition — he bought sports equipment for local Mexican schools, gave poor people and teenagers jobs, and was more than generous to his country's police and feds. By 1987, he had 400 people, including high school students, working for him on both sides of the border.

Meanwhile, Fermin Arevalo, a former candelilla smuggler, started a marijuana plantation in El Mulato, a pueblo on the Mexican side of the Rio Grande near Lajitas. By 1984, Arevalo and Acosta, the two biggest drug mafiosi in Chihuahua, were out for each other's turf. One day Arevalo tried to ambush Acosta. But Acosta's men killed Arevalo instead, and rumor has it that Acosta then ritually mutilated Arevalo and stuffed his genitals in his mouth. The shootout happened in El Mulato. In Ojinaga, the nearest approximation of a city, Acosta took to strutting around sporting Uzis and AR15s. Teenaged boys, recruited into the business as runners, would show off their automatics, and the streets were riddled with shootouts.

Weisman talked with a school teacher in Ojinaga who bitterly lamented the slick, Miami Vice mentality that has lately destroyed traditional notions of work and morality. "Professor," the teacher remembered a student saying, "you are a *pendejo* (pubic hair). I make more in one night carrying a plastic bag across the Rio than you make all year."

"What can I tell them?" the teacher asked Weisman in despair. The schools were devoid of books, but in the rest of Ojinaga there was prosperity, bought at the price of its children imitating swaggering criminals.

In 1987, probably in response to the murder of DEA agent Enrique Camarena in Mexico, justice on both sides of the border apparently decided to finish off Acosta. Mexican officials surrounded his house and blew Acosta's brains out while Border Patrol helicopters hovered on the U.S. side of the Rio Grande, poised for mop up operations. This all happened in Santa Elena, a few hundred yards from a Big Bend campground and trading post where you can buy fudgesicles and sunblock.

With Arevalo and Acosta gone, local gossip reports that Colombian drug dealers have arrived in the Big Bend. Whoever is involved, business is apparently still booming, despite burgeoning numbers of Border Patrol and Customs agents, high tech planes, helicopters and surveillance blimps. The park area these days is described by some as an armed camp. But to bored teenagers surrounded by smuggled chewing gum inputs and make-believe towns, what does an armed camp mean? Is it anything besides a video screen? Is a gun different from a joy stick? A person more mortal than a Ninja Turtle?

Michael Heffley was fatally shot at a place on the Rio Grande about half way between Lajitas, the movie set, and El Mulato, where the real shootout between Acosta's and Arevalo's gangs occurred. The four boys who admitted to sniping at the tourists were from El Mulato, though one recently moved to Redford, a nearby U.S. village said to be farther from a metropolitan area than any other American town in the contiguous 48 states.

The boys told authorities they were deer hunting, that they smoked some reefer, shot at a hawk, then spied the tourists on the raft. One boy, described by his Redford public school principal as quiet and nice, allegedly hollered "Let's shoot at the people." The *Houston Chronicle* later said he yelled, "Let's shoot at the gringos."

Things being how they are nowadays in the Big Bend, if the boy really targeted "the gringos," he probably did it less as an act of conscious defiance than as one of sporting deference. In a land of few people and even fewer Anglos, the gringo owns the candelilla, the ghost towns, the movie sets. The gringo flies the Blackhawk helicopters and the Aerostat blimps. The gringo dubs subtitles onto movies like *Deliverance*, for rent at the *cinevideos* of Ojinaga and Presidio. The gringo treks to the desert from Dallas, Houston, Australia, Berlin, and Midland-Odessa — from nowhere — and leaves never to be seen again. The gringo looks like the brawny men in the video game "Contra," the one where the brown people are puny and the big blondes score high, as long as you feed them quarters. The gringo buys the dope. Or he rafts down the rivers, 300 feet below a canyon rim, with a designer windbreaker and a gourmet box lunch. The gringo is Superman, Wyatt Earp, even Mr. T. He's all powerful, all image. If you zap him, he'll bounce right back. Or you can press rewind and go back to the start of the game.

In his chapter on the Big Bend, Weisman concludes: "The boundary between morality and depravity intersects at *la frontera*. At their junction, narcotics and weapons pour between the Americas. The political division itself adds to their value. Danger heightens and profits increase. As they do, hopes decline and drag the future along with them."

River-rafting tourists have been sniped at from the Mexican side of the Big Bend several times in recent years. 1988 was the first time anyone was hit. With Michael Heffley's death, we are reminded that Weisman is right — the unspoiled frontier is a fiction. And while hope declines, the children of the border stare across it, with cross-hatched eyes, point-blank.

— 1989

Sex, the Devil,
and Daycare

The sexual victimization of children is a major problem that until recently has remained largely hidden from national consciousness. One reason for the longtime silence on this issue is that children have been denied a voice in court. But the current wave of Satanic-day-care-molester trials has nothing to do with protecting kids.

If this society were really interested in doing that job, it would start with incest. Overwhelmingly, when children are molested, the culprits are fathers, stepfathers, mothers' boyfriends, brothers, and funny uncle types. Every day, thousands of cases of incestuous sexual abuse are reported nationally and hundreds prosecuted. Meanwhile, a mere 1.7 per cent of all reported child abuse—including beatings and neglect—is committed by teachers or other paid caretakers not related to the child. And of that minuscule proportion, only one-tenth is thought to involve sexual abuse.

On the surface it seems odd that day-care workers have become the most notorious molesters when, in fact, they're the rarest of the species. But when it comes to the issue of child sexual abuse, day-care workers are not meant to be facts. They've become symbols, products of a century's worth of American social and political history that has lately culminated in a new body of thought concerning children, child molesters, and ways of dealing with both that often go against both common sense and civil liberties. That much of this new theory comes from right-wing pro-family moralists is hardly surprising. That it is just as much a project of liberals is perhaps less obvious. But that feminists have been equally involved might seem downright weird without a history lesson to help sort out these strange bedfellows.

Child abuse has only recently achieved the status of a "national problem." A century ago, with "spare the rod and spoil the child" the prevailing maxim, the only cases of violence that got into courts or newspapers were the most bizarre ones—chaining kids to beds for weeks on end, for instance. More common assaults, like beatings, were chalked up to "discipline," the family's (particularly the father's) prerogative.

Neglect was another matter. Before the Progressive era, children were often removed from their homes if they were lacking food, clothing, and attention simply because the whole family was dirt-poor. In many states, destitution was included in the same statutes that outlawed neglect and cruelty to children. Turn-of-the-century reformers and social workers, mostly women, first publicized cruelty as a social rather than private problem. They focused on efforts to subsidize indigent mothers and outlaw child labor. By the New Deal, they had gotten the laws they wanted. The issue of violence against children, never well delineated to begin with, went into hibernation.

Then, in the 1960s, after several years of findings reported by radiologists and doctors in hospital emergency rooms, child abuse was rediscovered by the media and redefined to mean mainly assaults like beatings and scaldings in boiling hot bathtubs. Sociologists, after they had managed to draw arbitrary lines between abuse and spanking, noted that abuse occurred more among the poor—and therefore people of color—than among the middle and upper classes, who of course tended to be white. This fact became problematic when liberal legislators like Walter Mondale tried in the early 1970s to get money to fight child abuse. Conservatives upheld laissez faire and the privacy of the family; they refused to support anything that smacked of '60s-style social welfare programs. The liberals therefore chose to turn child abuse into a classless, apple-pie-and-motherhood issue by presenting it as an individual rather than political-economic pathology. When they were successful, they got the money to institute mandatory reporting laws and do some research on the problem. But it was tough to keep portraying abuse of children the same way AA does alcoholism. Especially because during regional or national economic down-turns, people had a tendency to step up the beatings. Too many uncomfortable questions were being raised that went far beyond scalding bathtubs.

From this perspective, the issue of sex with children has an important advantage: experts agree that it's committed by as many nice, comfortable white people as by disreputable welfare types. While studying incest, however, researchers were forced to acknowledge that it is very common—so much so that it seems practically endemic to the family as a social formation. Thus, any discussion of how to treat incest victims or how to punish offenders calls into question America's most hallowed institution.

The people who have stared most unflinchingly at the glaring connection between sexual abuse and the patriarchal nuclear family have been feminists. They have examined power arrangements inside the family, then shown how child-battering, wife battering, and incest are linked to extramural violence like rape. But in the Reaganite '80s, feminist consciousness-raising about sexual violence hasn't led to a critique of the family; rather it has encouraged moralism against evil people and narrowly legalistic remedies. Conservatives in Congress have successfully opposed funding for child abuse prevention and other child welfare programs. Instead, under the conservative-sponsored "Child Victim Witness Protection Act," states have received federal money to change their criminal codes. Armed with model statutes from the American Bar Association, legislators have put new laws on the books that aim to bring children into court to testify about sexual abuse and pornography even if it means contradicting a basic tenet of U.S. justice—that findings of fact must be made by rational "adult-like" individuals—which by definition almost always excludes tiny children.

The people preparing the cases—D.A.s, cops and child protective workers—find that sharing the incest accommodation syndrome theory and its axiom that kids never lie about sexual abuse makes their work a lot easier. And cooperation among all these people has clearly functioned to defend the family rather than question it. El Paso sexual abuse social worker Yolanda Aguilar, for instance, says the techniques used by her agency, the Texas Department of Human Services, usually sway an incest abuser into admitting what he did during the first interview. "These cases are easiest to prosecute," she says, but adds that she almost always recommends to the court that the offender get probation and treatment. "Most of these people really do love their kids," she says. The men—and children—are often immediately returned to the home.

Meanwhile, the traditional American family continues to be squeezed by an onslaught of postcapitalist pressures, from burgeoning consumerism to reproductive technology to economic recession and its by-product, the two-income home. People sense all this, whether consciously or not, but it seems that the weaker the family gets, the holier is its image. How, then, to denounce child sexual victimization without committing blasphemy?

The times demand a scapegoat, and what better one than daycare? If the private family is sacred, the public child-care center is profane. If stay-at-home mothers are holy, then the people they pay to take care of their kids when they escape from the house are witches.

Day-care hysteria is another instance of how conservatives have cornered the market these days, supplying fundamentalist rhetoric for a public trying to sort out worry and puzzlement over deep-seated social changes. All this is going on in a climate of free-floating erotophobia. When you consider AIDS, for example, the right would rather you think of the confessional and abstinence than condoms and Clorox. When you ponder leaving your children in day-care, you're supposed to focus on the sexual evil of your selfishness.

It's not surprising either that Satanism is a motif when day-care teachers are accused of molesting. The Devil, after all, has been linked with filthy lucre at least since Luther. And these days, whether it's mothers agonizing about going out to work or day-care operators trying to make a return on their investment, raising kids is increasingly caught up in the undisguised cash nexus.

For right-wing fundamentalists, the profit motive satanized becomes Pornography. And ironically, recent feminist antiporn campaigns, though secular, dovetail perfectly with conservative devil-mongering. Fundamentalists hate pornography because love on top of the sheets and outside marriage is wrong. Feminists like Women Against Pornography hate it because they think that it breeds violence against women and exploits female models, and that women cannot possibly enjoy the fantasies porn portrays: by definition, they are victims of male voyeurism, patriarchal culture, violence, implicit rape.

Both fundamentalists and feminists have aroused controversy when attacking people's First Amendment right to publish and read any damn thing they please. But battling kiddie-porn is much easier. These days, few people want to consider the fact that children have their own sexual life, which may include attractions toward adults and fantasy with sexual motifs that can even take sadomasochistic forms. Maybe you can argue that adult women have such thoughts, but kids, everyone agrees, are pure.

So if kids say they've had sexual contact with adults, believe them, always. The insistence that "Children never lie" stems partly from collective guilt over the time when they were hardly ever believed. But some feminists totally reject the idea that sexual victimization is ever imagined. They think Freud was cravenly shielding men when he said his women patients who remembered childhood incest were merely embellishing their Oedipus complexes. And if women never merely imagine such perversions, then neither do children.

On the other hand, the whole argument about whether children fantasize sex with adults may be obsolete, since they are exposed to so much literal information about it nowadays. Homes are filled with the phantasmagoric sexuality of MTV. And there is school. One El Paso psychiatrist recently treated a whole family whose 11-year-old daughter had accused her father of molesting her. The father at first vehemently denied it, but finally copped a plea which involved going into therapy. After months of treatment, the daughter very eloquently admitted that she'd made the accusation because her father was an alcoholic. She thought that if she said he'd molested her he would have to spend the weekend in jail and away from the bottle. She said she got the idea after studying "Good Touch Bad Touch" in health class. She was in sixth grade, but preschoolers are getting the same lessons.

The family never went back to court, but if they had, the State would likely have refused to believe the daughter's new story. They probably would have called it "recanting." And if children like her never lie the first time, there is no particular reason why the adults they accuse merit such legal niceties as corroborating evidence, proofs of the children's competency, or even a requirement that they show up in court during a trial.

Because much of this thinking has been expressed in feminist rhetoric, a final convolution as it percolates into the hinterlands is the "You've come a long way, baby" thesis. Social workers and prosecutors on child-saving jihads are saying women can do anything men can. Including, in the case described in the following pages, viciously molest children.

— *1987*

The Making of a
Modern Witch Trial

On Halloween night, 1985, police pulled up to a party that Gayle Stickler Dove was attending at the zoo in El Paso, Texas. Dove, then 41, worked afternoons as a volunteer zoo keeper; mornings she earned money teaching four-year-olds at the East Valley Family YMCA day-care center and preschool. As TV cameras rolled, the police handcuffed Dove, put her in a squad car, and proceeded to the house of 36-year-old Michelle "Mickey" Noble, another Y teacher. She wasn't home — her attorney had advised her to stay at a friend's. Next day she turned herself in.

The charges, multiple counts of aggravated sexual assault and indecency with a child, alleged that Dove and Noble, under the pretext of taking their classes to a nearby park on sunny days, had instead walked them to Noble's home, where they fondled the kids' genitals and had the kids touch theirs; stuck pencils and syringes up the anuses and penises of little boys; helped an unknown male

---

NOTE: Little would be accomplished by changing the names of the accused in this story — they've already been splashed across so many front pages and TV screens that anonymity now is impossible. As for the children, since this article was first published, I've come to realize that many of them truly believe they were sexually abused by their teachers. The difference in suffering experienced by an actual rape victim and by someone who merely believes herself to be victimized may well be no difference at all. For that reason, I've assigned pseudonyms to everyone directly involved, except for attorneys, police, social workers, and the defendants.

rape a three-year-old girl; photographed the children defecating; terrified them into silence by sawing open stuffed animals; and did much of this while wearing monster masks. Convicted and sent to prison, Noble and Dove swear they're innocent. So do their families, friends, and a plethora of reporters, psychologists, private investigators, and others who got involved in their cases.

If this story sounds familiar, it's because there has been a nationwide rash of similar cases in the wake of the notorious McMartin preschool scandal in suburban Los Angeles. McMartin, which first became public in August 1983, escalated to 207 counts of child molestation against seven defendants, including the school's wheelchair-bound, septuagenarian woman owner. Though charges against her and four others have been dropped, two teachers are currently on trial for several counts remaining from hundreds of children's stories that they were forced to sacrifice animals, desecrate churches, pillage corpses from graveyards, fornicate on the shoulders of busy highways, and play games like "naked movie star."

A month after McMartin surfaced, authorities in Jordan, Minnesota, got some run-of-the-mill reports that a local resident was molesting children. A snowballing probe led to arrests of 23 other adults charged with victimizing children by practicing ritual sadism and murder. Two people were acquitted and charges against everyone else but the original defendant were dropped. The following summer, several new investigations started. A preschool teacher in Niles, Michigan, was accused (and later convicted) of molesting a four-year-old boy while snapping off the head of a chicken. In Memphis, four preschool teachers were indicted for wearing masks and robes while burning children with candles, locking them in cages, and baptizing them in the name of the devil. In Miami, the director of a babysitting service and her husband were convicted of abuse after children testified about anal rape with a crucifix, masks, slaughtered parakeets, and feces eating. In Malden, Massachusetts, a day-care teacher was convicted of abuse, indecent assault, and rape after nine children testified that the teacher wore a clown suit and took them to a "magic room," and one said that he killed birds and squirrels. At West Point, the FBI spent a year probing the army's child development center and concluded there were indications of abuse that others termed "ritualized" and "satanic." In Maplewood, New Jersey, after an investigation beginning in June 1985, day-care teacher Kelly Michaels was indicted and is currently on trial for allegedly assaulting children with silver-ware, dressing in a black robe, playing the piano in the nude, and us-ing urine, feces, bloody tampons, and peanut butter and jelly in her molestations.

As "junior McMartins," most of these cases have been little pub-licized. But they are perhaps even more compelling than their splashy California precursor precisely because, unsung and hidden in the sub-urbs and hinterlands, they represent something new and epidemic in this country. The child accusers and their parents are almost invari-ably white and middle class. So are the people they accuse. And of-ten, the alleged perpetrators are women, themselves parents — in short, the last people you'd associate with sleazy trench-coated pe-dophiles.

Dove, for instance, is the mother of a teenage daughter and wife of a high school band instructor. Mildly overweight, she camouflages matronliness with the kind of makeup and medium-length, wavy blond coiffure you expect to see on a friendly but no-nonsense small-town waitress. Dove used to attend all her husband's band competi-tions to help root for the students. She has won awards for her volun-teer work at the Humane Society animal shelter, and her house used to be filled with strays. That, of course, was before she was arrested.

Mickey Noble, who wore her brown hair in a curlier version of Diane Keaton's in *Manhattan*, has two children, nine and 14, and is married to an envelope salesman. When the family lived in Kansas and needed two incomes, she took a job at a day-care center so she could enroll her own kids and be with them. She also taught Sunday school. According to her mother, Noble is soft-spoken, almost meek. She has little interest in politics and probably has never voted. Her whole world revolved around her family, church, and neighborhood.

Noble's mother, Dorothy Davis, says her daughter thought a while before accepting the Y teaching job — it only paid minimum wage and the Nobles didn't really need the money, but an acquain-tance who worked at the Y convinced Noble she might as well get paid for the kind of things she spent so much time doing as a volun-teer at her son's and daughter's schools. According to her mother, "Miss Mickey" used to spend hours after supper drawing her own sketches for the preschoolers to color next day, or popping popcorn to use for blossoms on construction paper tree projects.

All these facts were later discussed in the community and in the courtroom. They were said to prove something about what kind of people molest other people's children. All they really proved, though, was that Noble and her colleague Dove were indistinguishable from everyone else with a never-even-had-a-traffic-ticket background — including the assistant D.A. who tried them and who insists the two women are the lowest form of life.

As another assistant D.A. put it, "They had their day in court." But what does that mean these days if you're accused of being a day-care child molester? In El Paso or anywhere else?

The consensus among experts is that sexual abuse isn't increasing relative to the number of children in this country, but media focus on the issue, and reporting laws passed in every state during the 1970s, have resulted in skyrocketing reports of child sexual abuse nationally. In 1978 only 12,000 cases were reported. In 1986, depending on which of several agencies you consulted, there were 100,000 to 200,000.

El Paso's Department of Human Resources, since renamed the Department of Human Services, began a specialized child sexual abuse unit in 1983, in the wake of exploding national concern about the problem. In Texas and every other state, doctors, teachers and others who deal professionally with kids are now legally bound to call a child protection office or a hotline if they suspect a child has been victimized. Reports from the general public can be made anonymously: the assumption is that you wouldn't accuse someone of such a disgusting act unless you sincerely thought it happened. As of last spring the El Paso unit had gotten about 1500 reports, mostly alleging incest by men and boys against little girls; about half a dozen of the reported molesters were women.

On Saturday morning, February 16, 1985, DHR took a call from Steven Garcia. Garcia was worried that someone was molesting his two-and-a-half-year old son Eric. Eric told his parents that "someone at the Y was taking his pants off, playing games in the bathroom, playing doggy, licking someone's face and chest, playing doctor, and tickling hineys," the intake worker wrote.

A few days later Garcia's wife, Darleen, called: she was sure the molesters her son Eric was talking about worked at the YMCA where he attended morning preschool. According to Darleen, these employees included "Ms. Dove," who kissed Eric's "boobies" and "peepee," "Miss Jane" (a teacher's aid), who stuck her finger in his "hiney," "Ms.

Mickey," who kissed his boobies, and "Ms. Carole" (also an aide), who grabbed him "down there." The case was assigned to DHR worker Helga Wright.

Subsequently, Darleen reported that on Saturday, Eric had gone into a frenzied trance, rubbed his penis, gotten an erection, grabbed his testicles, tried to lick his stomach and penis, then started yelling names. Whose names, exactly? According to Wright's notes, Darleen told her Eric said, "This is what Miss Mickie" — Wright's spelling — "does, give me the penny, I want you to touch my hiney." But other notes survive, which Darleen would later testify she spontaneously wrote right after Eric talked about being molested. Besides Miss Carol and Miss Dove, they mention a family babysitter named Stephanie, who was, in fact, the first person Eric had named. She "plays doctor and snake, she bites me on the neck, she takes off my pants and puts pennies on my peepee," Darleen wrote. Next day and the day after, Eric continued to talk about "what Stephanie does to me."

Darleen was distraught; Wright was doubtful. At an office interview February 20 with Eric and his parents, she noted that the little boy would not say if anyone had ever touched his "private parts" until "his parents and I asked specific questions, such as, "Did Miss Mickie kiss your boobies?" Eric answered in the affirmative to all the items regarding Miss Jane, Miss Mickie, Miss Dove but only after prompting. I explained...that asking this kind of leading question is not the usual method of interviewing alleged victims. My reason for doing so was the parents' frustration and their concern that they would not be believed."

Next day, Darleen reported that Eric said that someone named Ricardo or Richard spanked him and also put his hand in Eric's "hiney." Darleen thought Eric was referring to the janitor at the Y. She also told Wright that for some time, Eric had been refusing to "go potty" and sometimes had accidents. He was constipated, having nightmares, and was afraid of the Big Bad Wolf. He said a man with a saw was in the ceiling and was going to saw his tummy — Miss Mickey said so. And Richard spanked him.

The following week Wright did a home visit with the Garcias. This time, she noted some background, including that Steven was a U.S. Border Patrol agent who had recently been transferred from New Mexico to El Paso. At the time they moved, Steven had gone on the night shift, meaning Eric was seeing much less of his dad than he was used to. The Garcias rented a house owned by the family's minister, whose daughter was Stephanie, the babysitter. A month later, Wright would interview Stephanie and comment, "She appears mentally slow...I was unable to form an opinion regarding Stephanie's care or abuse of Eric."

Even though Eric once said that Wright herself had spanked him, Darleen fixed completely on the Y. "She does not believe he is confusing his teachers with others and thinks everything that is done at the Y is done to cover up the abuse and scare the children," Wright noted. She suggested that Eric see a therapist. When a psychologist interviewed Eric and Darleen, Eric never mentioned any sexual abuse during open-ended questioning, and the psychologist noted that "there was no indication of anxiety" by Eric — "However, there was much anxiety" demonstrated by Darleen. The therapist thought Eric might be having flashbacks about an incident of abuse that happened long ago.

Meanwhile, the Garcias pulled Eric out of the Y and were infuriated that DHR wouldn't shut down the day-care center. During March and April, agency workers went there to interview the people Eric had named. Day-care director Karron Wilson was offended by the child's allegations — she trusted her staff completely and now felt they were afraid even to touch the kids. Dove, according to DHR notes, was "angry and feels victimized." Noble remembered how Eric wouldn't even go to the bathroom the first month he'd been at the Y, and just before Christmas she had to change his underwear and wipe him after he "pooped in his pants during lunch and smelled." She thought Eric's talk of her sticking her fingers in his "hiney" could have come from that incident.

Noble says she couldn't believe what was happening at first, and told Wilson she wanted to quit her job to protect herself. But Wilson said quitting would only make Noble look guilty, and besides, the children needed her because she was such a good teacher. Noble says Wilson told her that if the case ever ended up in court, the Y would back her up and provide her with an attorney. (Wilson now refuses to comment.) So Noble continued to teach during the spring of 1985.

Wright returned to the Y unannounced several times and never saw any children demonstrating fear toward any teachers. DHR then asked about a dozen parents to bring their kids in for interviews designed to ferret out signs of sexual abuse. Of those, four went through a session with "anatomically correct" dolls. No records of the interviews were included in the trial's discovery material, but Wright's earlier conversations with parents and their children indicate that she asked if anyone had "touched their privates." Some parents were also read a laundry list of "symptoms or symptom clusters which can be indicative of any possible sexual abuse."

Many YMCA preschoolers' parents had work and social connections with each other. One taught the children at the Y, another taught exercise classes, another was on the Y's board of directors, and others were these people's neighbors and relatives. During that spring, many learned through the grapevine about the investigation of Noble and Dove, and about what to start looking for in the children. In April, DHR closed out the investigation after declaring its findings inconclusive. But whether alarmed parents stopped interrogating their children is another question.

> Social Worker: You said you saw some monsters someplace.
> Mike: I didn't see any monsters anywhere.
> Social Worker: Well, when you were at Miss Mickey's house, did you see some there?
> Mike: Let me go see if (inaudible) is here.
> Social Worker: No, no, no. We have to sit and talk. When you were at Miss Mickey's house, were there monsters there? The other day you said something about monsters in the hallway.
> Mike: Where at?
> Social Worker: At Miss Mickey's house.
> Mike: I didn't go inside. I didn't see any.
> Social Worker: You didn't see any? You said you didn't go inside?
> Mike: Uh-uh.
> Social Worker: But you told us you did.
> Mike: Well, I made a lie, and they didn't.

> *Videotape transcript, the State of Texas*
> *v. Michelle Elaine Noble.*

Nationally, some 65 per cent of last year's sexual abuse reports turned out to be unfounded, and El Paso's percentage is about equal. Many experts are disturbed by this figure. In an era of federal cutbacks in funding for all kinds of services for children, many who are serious-

ly or fatally injured through actual abuse are already known to protective agencies that lack the resources to rescue them. Every dollar
wasted on checking false allegations, therefore, is that much less to
spend on fighting the real thing.

For Yolanda Aguilar, the social worker who headed El Paso's sexual abuse unit at the time Steven Garcia phoned in his complaint,
false reporting "comes with the territory" — her people can handle it.
These days, along with the usual reports of incest in intact families,
the hotline is full of accusations made by children and mothers involved in divorce cases and custody battles. Many of these, Aguilar
says, are malicious inventions of vengeful ex-spouses. "But you look
at the mother's affect and the child's spontaneity in relating what
happened. You can tell when they've been rehearsed."

The lies she hears over the hotline as marriages break up are
something new for Aguilar. Like just about every worker in the child
protection field, she cut her teeth on incest in stable families with
constellations of parents, siblings, grandparents, and perhaps uncles.
Also like most child protection people, she applies prevailing theories
about incestuous relationships in her work with kids and their relatives. According to a decade's worth of literature on incest, children
don't lie about it. If a girl says grandpa, daddy, or uncle had sex with
her, she isn't likely to be making it up. But often, after she has come
forward with the accusation, she'll back off and recant in a desperate
attempt to keep her family from shattering or her father from going to
jail. This behavior represents the "incest accommodation syndrome,"
according to a theory developed by California psychiatrist Roland
Summit. The idea is that if the girl says it happened, the concerned
social worker or therapist will stand up for her, believing her. If she
later recants, you should show you care by not believing her.

After untold years of hardly anyone believing children who said
they were molested, the theory is compelling. But when it is used to
influence court cases and criminal trials, it raises disturbing questions.
In the McMartin case and its mini-versions, hundreds of children
have offered vague, garbled, contradictory horror stories with virtually no physical evidence to back them up. After repeated questioning,
many children have admitted they lied. But in the minds of many
protective service people, they have merely "recanted." Although
these cases are not about incest and don't involve the same pressures
to keep a family secret, the presumptions of the incest accommoda-

tion syndrome theory are applied: believe the child, however sketchy the evidence, and never take no for an answer.

The first week of June, about a month after preschool closed for the summer, Richard Moreno — like Steven Garcia a Border Patrol agent — went to the El Paso police and reported what his three-year-old daughter, Patti, had told him a few days earlier. According to Richard, Patti was watching her brothers play when she uttered something that sounded like "fuching." After Richard repeatedly asked Patti where she'd heard this, she said that Miss Mickey "said it all the time" at her house. Richard said Patti told him she had gone there three times with other classmates. She then began talking of having makeup applied at Noble's and of seeing people there dressed up as monsters, brandishing masks and swords. Richard also said Patti told him Miss Mickey "kissed" and "tapped" her on her genitals, a black mailman kissed her, and a policeman chopped off a baby's head. He reported that Francie, his wife, an aerobics teacher at the Y, had questioned Patti further that evening, and the little girl added that a Daddy monster had showered with her and had shampooed and blow-dried her hair.

A few days later the police took Patti to the hospital to have her genitals examined. During the exam, a doctor later testified, the little girl acted terrified and screamed, "Please don't hurt me like he did." The doctor found a ruptured hymen; he later testified that it appeared Patti had been penetrated. He was virtually certain she could not have done it herself.

During the next few days the case snowballed. DHR immediately reopened the Eric Garcia file, brought the police into the investigation, and spread the word to out-of-town agencies that something big was going on in El Paso. Soon calls were returned by experts like an FBI agent with the Sexual Exploitation of Children Task Force in New York City, who offered DHR a list of things to look for in day-care sex abuse cases. The FBI's list was big on nightmares, constipation, pencil penetration, pictures being taken, keeping secrets, and playing "silly games." A child protective services worker from the Fort Worth area suggested the El Paso people look for monsters, masks, dressing up, or going on field trips.

Armed with these suggestions, DHR worker Marina Gallardo and police Youth Services Division Detective Sergio Cox set out to visit the children who'd been in Noble's and Dove's classes. That they went as a team was peculiar, since traditionally, police and social workers do different types of work. Social workers don't normally go around hunting up child victims; they only interview after kids have been brought to them. Since they are not in the business of gathering evidence for a criminal case, it may sometimes be appropriate for social workers to refuse to take no for an answer as they interview a child about what happened to her. This is especially true when the police already have a confession or corroboration that sexual assault did indeed occur. As for the cops, they are the ones who are supposed to be inherently skeptical of witnesses' stories, not automatically believe something happened. They're not supposed to be leading.

Nevertheless, Gallardo and Cox visited homes together. After a bit of icebreaking chitchat about HeMan, they took turns asking the children specific, yes-no questions, like whether they had nightmares, were afraid of monsters, had ever been to Miss Mickey's house or played "secret games." Some of the kids said they'd been to Miss Mickey's — like Abel Luna, a student of Dove's who said he'd seen a Christmas tree and eaten her cookies. Abel's younger cousin David, barely three years old, also went to Y preschool. Cox and Gallardo told both boys' mothers that the children had probably been molested and that they should take them in for medical exams and file criminal complaints.

But even though both boys were taken to DHR offices and put through sessions with the anatomically correct dolls, "The children were not real responsive" to social worker or police questioning, says David's mother, Lucia Luna. "David wasn't even three yet anyway so he hardly had sufficient vocabulary." She says neither of the boys ever demonstrated any behavioral changes, so she and her sister concluded they had not been abused and politely stopped returning Cox and Gallardo's calls.

Four-year-old Sergio Abbud was another student in Dove's class. When Cox and Gallardo came to the Abbud home they asked Sergio a spate of leading questions, first in English, then in Spanish, such as "Did your teacher ever pull your underwear down?" Sergio answered "'no', just like they'd asked him if he'd ever been to Mars," remembers his mother, Guadalupe.

But for every family like the Lunas or the Abbuds, there were others who concluded over the summer that the worst had indeed happened. Some kids answered "yes" to Cox and Gallardo's questions about whether they feared monsters. Some were having nightmares. Whenever a child shied away from Cox after he said he was a cop and displayed his gun, the detective told the parents "Noble and Company" had used police uniforms to terrorize the kids so they wouldn't reveal they'd been molested.

Like Sergio Abbud and the Luna children, four-year-old Jennifer Cooley said nothing in particular. But Cox and Gallardo told her parents what sex acts they were looking for and who was supposed to have done them. They also recited the behavioral symptoms list. During the next month, according to Jennifer's father, "We were... kind of on the lookout...just to make sure" nothing had happened to Jennifer. The Cooleys said they even started taking notes on her behavior.

Finally, one evening a month after Cox and Gallardo's visit, Jennifer said to her father, "Let's take a shower." Cooley became upset because "my daughter is not supposed to be talking sexy to me." He testified that he asked her where she got that idea and Jennifer replied, "Me and Miss Mickey took a shower" at Miss Mickey's (later she changed it to a bath), and the Dukes of Hazard were there, too. Within the next few hours, the Cooleys said, Jennifer had performed a belly dance, described lying in Miss Mickey's bed with Patti, and thrust her hips up and down on the floor.

Then there was Lee Irigoyen, who had always been fond of his teacher, Miss Dove. Lee's father, Frank, is a retired cop who once worked in Youth Protective Services, as Cox does now. Lee's mother, Pamela, is a first grade public school teacher. She is also the sister of one of the Y preschool teachers and the cousin of another's husband. Pamela's sister had told her during the spring about the first sex abuse investigation at the Y. Now it was July, and she came home to find Cox and Gallardo's business cards on the door. When Pamela called them and heard the details of the new investigation, she and Frank were shocked, and spent a week worrying about their son before Cox and Gallardo returned to the house. Cox showed his police badge and gun to Lee, asked him to sit in the living room, and told the parents to wait in the hall. Pamela said she and Frank were "extremely nervous." What happened then isn't clear. Frank later testified that Cox and Gallardo never led Lee by suggesting any particular sexual act; that only when Lee began talking about "secret games" did Cox call Frank in and tell him to take over the questioning.

But Cox testified that Lee's negative answers about sex abuse constituted "avoidance behavior." So when Cox couldn't get the desired response he says he called Frank and told him exactly what he and Gallardo were looking for. "I said (to Frank) 'you see the line of questions we're asking, and where we're coming from. You try.'"

According to Frank, Lee then talked of playing the "puppy dog game," where the kids would get down on all fours and lick Dove's and Noble's "boobies." Frank said Lee pulled up his shirt to demonstrate. He also claimed that the little boy later said Miss Mickey and Miss Dove "stuck a pencil in my rectum."

Suddenly a lot of Lee's behavior during the last several months started making sense. Frank remembered, for instance, that lately Lee didn't want to rough-house with his dad as much as he used to. He had also been wetting the bed and having nightmares since the fall of 1984 (though Pamela thought the problems didn't start until the spring of 1985). There had been a lot of sickness in the Irigoyen family — Frank was in and out of hospitals with a bone infection and Lee's aunt was dying of breast cancer. She was the second of Pamela's sisters to be fatally ill, and Pamela was away from home at her bedside almost every night during the spring after the first DHR investigation. One night when his parents told him that his aunt was never going to get well, Lee began screaming, "I don't want you and Dad to die!" During this same period, he began sitting quietly in his room before dinner and coloring, which according to his parents was unprecedented.

Now it all fell into place — every inexplicable or troubling thing Lee did could be chalked up to sexual molestation.

Throughout the summer it seemed that everybody Noble and Dove knew was interviewed — everybody but Noble and Dove. Though the police normally question the suspects at some point in an investigation, Cox seemed to studiously avoid any contact with the two teachers. They knew they were being investigated because the Cox and Gallardo team was calling on their employers, neighbors, and friends.

DHR and police reports of these visits paint a bleak picture of creeping fear and suspicion. One report reads that Wilson, the day-care director who Noble says pleaded with her not to quit her job, "stated that at first she did not believe what Miss Mickey was doing, but after talking with Sandra Fredricks (executive director of the Y and grandmother of one of the child accusers), she believes." In another report, Cox wrote, "Mr. Fulton (director of the El Paso Zoo)...further stated that he couldn't believe that Dove is the type of person that would molest children, 'however you just don't know nowadays.'"

As the summer wore on Noble became reclusive and started crying a lot. "She wouldn't go out of the house, even to go to the supermarket," her mother says. "She thought everybody knew who she was." In mid-August, a TV station got wind of the investigation and ran pictures of the police reports, complete with Noble's name and address. "Fifteen minutes later, she started getting the first obscene calls and death threats," Davis says. Noble says she became a prisoner while she was still living in her house.

By early fall, Cox and Gallardo had interviewed 34 children and assembled a list of eight whose parents were willing to press charges. But what to show a jury? Almost the only conventionally admissible evidence was a doctor's testimony about one little girl's broken hymen and her terror (coupled with her pleas not to hurt her as "he" had). Otherwise, there was only the word of a bunch of adults about hearsay garnered from children scarcely out of diapers.

But there was some unconventional evidence — videotaped interviews of the children made by the DHR workers Gallardo and Aguilar and by Detective Cox. For the last few years the Texas Department of Human Services has followed a national trend of recording interviews of alleged victims of sexual abuse — particularly children under 12. The original purpose of video taping was to preserve a record that would help plan appropriate therapy, and confront the children with their original stories if they later denied it. Also, it's said that making the accused sit through an audiovisual display of a child's tale of abuse often shames the perpetrator into telling the truth.

In 1983, Texas began permitting videos of children to be used in courts as evidence in criminal cases. Traditionally, the law had recognized only a few types of secondhand testimony, but the new video exception to the rules prohibiting hearsay was meant to spare the child the trauma of sitting in a courtroom filled with scary adults and the person accused of assaulting her. Videos in court are controversial, since they arguably violate U.S. and state constitutional guarantees that the accused shall have the right to confront witnesses against them — which traditionally has meant those witnesses must physically face the accused as they testify. In the summer of 1987, the Texas Court of Criminal Appeals ruled videotaped testimony unconstitutional. During Noble's trial, though, only a few lower courts in other parts of the state had made the same ruling, and in El Paso, tapes made solely by the prosecution were still admissible.

Apart from the questionable constitutionality of using videotapes at all, those done for the Noble/Dove case raise another issue, that of the children's "competency." To take the stand in Texas, a child must prove she is "competent," which means rational and mature enough to independently recall what she's testifying about. She has to be able to remember what she witnessed and tell her own story about it, not someone else's version. She must also show she knows the difference between the truth and a lie, promise to tell only the truth in court, and somehow demonstrate that she knows she'll get into trouble if she breaks that promise.

When videotapes were still admissible, if the child was never called into court and only appeared on tape, competency did not have to be proved. But judging from the Noble/Dove tapes, many of the preschooler plaintiffs were not qualified to testify under any circumstances. Typical is the video made of Patti Moreno shortly before she underwent the exam that revealed her ruptured hymen. The tapes starts with Aguilar questioning the little girl to see if she knows the difference between the truth and a lie. After Patti proves unable to tell what either of these words mean, Aguilar points to an orange chair and asks what color it is.

"Orange," Patti answers.

"Orange," repeats Aguilar. "If I tell you it's green, is that a truth or a lie?"

"True."

"It's true?...If I tell you it's snowing in here, is that true, or is it a lie?"

"True."

"It's true? It's snowing in here? Oh, is must be cold in here. My goodness...."

But even when the children proved incompetent, the interviewers continued rolling the tapes. Because the children had virtually nothing to volunteer, pressure was applied though various means to get them to talk. There was supplication mixed with veiled threats, as when Jennifer Cooley's mother sat in the interview room and begged, "Did you know Detective Cox is looking at you on TV? So you've got to talk." There was total refusal to accept "no" answers, as when Cox displayed his gun and handcuffs during the following exchange with one child:

"Who went to that party…?"

"I don't know…I don't know."

"Oh, you do too know."

"I do not."

"Yeah you do."

There was flattery, as when Gallardo cajoled, "And I know they scared you and they did it so you wouldn't talk. But I know you're brave and I know you're pretty smart too and you know the only way that we can help you is for you to tell."

Even in the face of these interrogations, most of the children, maddeningly enough, insisted on going about their business pedaling bikes around the video room or talking about crayons while the frustrated interviewers chalked it up to "avoidance behavior." Patti, a tiny, shy little girl, seemed polite and eager to please Yolanda Aguilar, but answered most questions with "I forgot." Aguilar pressed on and on, and Patti finally started crying. Aguilar cradled Patti in her arms, handed her a doll with genitals and asked some more. Patti then buried her face in Aguilar's bosom and closed her eyes. "Patti is going to sleep," Aguilar said, and stopped the camera. Later, in court, she said the child was terrorized. But to anyone viewing the videotape, it seems equally reasonable to assume Patti played possum so the big lady would bug off.

Why were the tapes made this way? One reason may be that the interviewers, who had little training, didn't know any better. The other reason, according to Gallardo, was that she and the other interviewers were instructed by Assistant D.A. Debra Kanof "not to worry about the legalities."

Kanof, then 32, was the former head of the Rape and Child Abuse Section of the El Paso County D.A.'s office when she first read the DHR and police reports about Eric Garcia. Fighting abuse isn't just a job for Kanof — it's a passion. She's on the board of the local chapter of the National Committee for the Prevention of Child Abuse, and also of the El Paso Shelter for Battered Women. She used to volunteer at the local rape crisis center, which is where she says she learned the art of talking to victims. With four-and-a-half years' experience doing child abuse cases, Kanof claims to be the most experienced prosecutor in the country.

Kanof, advocate of wives and children, is herself divorced, childless, and fiercely proud that she made it into the D.A.'s office, when 10 years ago "people said a woman couldn't stand up to the pressure of criminal court." A big, brash woman, she often cautions juries to judge only the legal merits of her prosecutions, not her loud delivery. Kanof's good friend Aguilar says that in court, Kanof is "like a lioness protecting her young" — a vast improvement over some of El Paso's former "good ole boy D.A.'s who wouldn't prosecute molesters because they said there wasn't corroborating evidence." As far as Aguilar's concerned, a child's word about such matters is corroborating evidence.

For her part, Kanof is an avid follower of Kee MacFarlane, whose child sexual abuse clinic in Los Angeles, Children's Institute International, interviewed all 400-plus children in the McMartin case. Social worker MacFarlane and her assistants told the McMartin kids they could be "junior detectives" by telling the "yukky secret," but would be dummies if they didn't admit they'd been molested by their teachers. After repeated interviewing produced statements about bizarre sex rituals in airplanes, hot air balloons, underground tunnels, graveyards, and funeral parlors, MacFarlane told the press that the McMartin preschool was part of a national network of kiddy pornographers and Satanists operating out of day-care centers.

She is not alone in believing in a Satanic porno conspiracy afoot throughout the country, even though worldwide searches by everyone from parents to the FBI have failed to uncover one dirty picture, barbecued baby body, or other incriminating object mentioned by the children who have been extensively interviewed following child molesting allegations. Lack of evidence doesn't seem to concern the Satanism proponents. Some believe everything the kids are saying to social workers and therapists is true. Many self-styled women's and children's advocates — Kanof, for example — denounce psychologists who say the children are fantasizing. She compares their attitude with that of Freud, whom she calls a male chauvinist for saying that Victorian-era women who reported childhood sex with their fathers were often hysterical. Jon Conte, who teaches at the University of Chicago's School of Social Service Administration, points out that common images of ritualistic, sexualized brutality crop up among children in widely scattered locations throughout the U.S. and Canada. He discounts mass hysteria as the cause because, he says, hysteria by definition occurs in rural, geographically isolated areas.

But Lee Coleman, a Berkeley psychiatrist and outspoken critic of the use of incest theories to deal with out-of-home molestation charges, believes Satanism is popping up in everyone's minds not because of what the children have experienced in common, but because the interviewers have all been through the same thing.

That child protective personnel are getting their imagery of abuse from common sources is clear. In 1986, for instance, a sex abuse conference in San Jose, California, featured Brad Darling, a sheriff's department lieutenant investigating an alleged Satanist ring in Bakersfield. Darling told his audience it was no coincidence that a large shipment of pesticide-laden watermelons came from the Bakersfield area. And how about the fact that the only African killer bees spotted in the entire country also were near Bakersfield? This, Darling implied, proved that Satanist molesters were organized within the "highest elements of society" and will stop at nothing to avenge themselves against child protection advocates. Roland Summit, theorist of the incest accommodation syndrome, sat in the audience adding supporting comments to Darling's presentation.

In the McMartin case, social worker MacFarlane's interviews with the kids elicited weird tales that went far beyond mutilated pets. The children's stories got so bizarre that in January 1985, Los Angeles D.A. Ira Reiner dropped all the hundreds of counts against five of the seven defendants. Reiner said the evidence against them was "incredibly weak."

Kanof says Reiner is "full of shit." She says that as soon as she saw the reports on Eric Garcia, she knew El Paso had its own McMartin case. She swears by MacFarlane's approach in McMartin, and keeps in touch with her by phone. Last year MacFarlane came to El Paso to address child protective workers. Aguilar says the focus of MacFarlane's talk reflected her recent writing in such publications as the University of Miami Law Review, in which she calls for unconventional interviewing methods that do "whatever it takes to get children to talk...." Kanof says she doesn't know if Noble and Dove were involved in Satanism. Aguilar says you might think some of the Y kids' stories, about being driven up mountains in fast race cars, or having their eyes removed and then reattached, seem absurd. But then, she says, with all the special visual and sound effects the entertainment industry pulls off these days, you never know what molesters can set up in their own houses to make children's stories sound unbelievable.

Still, it's clear that the Satanism hypothesis has made an impression on El Paso's sexual abuse unit. When a principal called to report a little girl unexplainably crying in class, DHS sent a worker out to the school. The child said she was upset because her mother had the family dog put to sleep. The mother, who is divorced, explained to the social worker that the dog had been suffering from degenerative liver disease. The social worker then canvassed the neighbors about whether the mother or any of her friends were involved in ritualistic animal slaughter.

As the Noble/Dove case progressed, Kanof not only interviewed the children herself, but also helped organize a support group for their parents that began in August and met weekly throughout the fall. The idea, she says, was to keep the parents "under control" so they wouldn't kill Noble and Dove. But in addition to support, the parents were regularly sharing their kids' latest stories about what their teachers had done to them. This might not have mattered so much in an ordinary case. But Texas was about to pass another extraordinary law tailored for child sex abuse cases. Commonly called an "outcry" exception to the rule forbidding hearsay, it allows the first adult the child tells about being molested to testify in place of the child.

"It's not really a new idea," explains Sam Callan, the district judge who ended up presiding over Noble's and Dove's trials. Callan says an older version of the "outcry" law was put on the books to help the state prosecute rape cases back when women were often too ashamed to go straight to the police and report a sexual assault. The woman might have told a friend about it, so her "outcry" was allowed into evidence, "just to verify she's told somebody, but not to prove the fact of the rape," the judge says.

But the new children's outcry law *would* be allowed to prove the fact of the sexual abuse allegation. A few weeks after it went into effect, Kanof went to the Grand Jury and indictments were handed down against Dove and Noble. Now social workers, doctors, police, mothers and fathers would be doing the testifying — the children weren't necessary. Suddenly there was a wave of new "outcries."

Several parents reported that their boys were talking about having plastic syringes stuck up their penises, and about having to defecate in front of video cameras. Defense attorneys protested that these "outcries" were inadmissible as evidence, coming as they did months after the children's original statements. But during preliminary hearings, Callan admitted them, as well as just about anything else Kanof requested.

Noble's lawyers didn't fare so well. The defense wanted to put on a psychologist who had minutely and statistically examined the tapes. He was prepared to testify that the "stress interrogation techniques" they revealed were similar to those used by the Cheka during the Moscow Trials, and by the Red Chinese on U.S. soldiers captured during the Korean War. He also wanted to suggest the similarity between the methods preserved on the video interviews and what hadn't been saved during the earliest unrecorded interviews of the children. Judge Callan, however, said he did not want to reduce the trial to an argument between experts. The jury had eyes and ears. They could watch the videotapes and decide for themselves, he said.

But could they? Even Callan was having a hard time. An elderly, white-haired gentleman who takes post-prandial siestas at his desk and enjoys quoting the Latin for maxims like "From novelty can come no good" in a West Texas drawl, Callan said after Noble's trial that he hates these cases, "never had anything like them before and don't know what to do with them. I just let Debbie (Kanof) shear the law off the page. An appeals court can rule later on what the law is."

Kanof denies it, but an employee of the law firm doing a multi-million-dollar civil suit brought by the parents against the Y says Kanof omitted a ninth child from her criminal case because his mother used to work for Callan and Kanof didn't want the judge disqualified from presiding. He was the perfect umpire for a no-holds-barred prosecution.

The first trial, Noble's, was held in March 1986, and played to an overflow crowd. As the jury and spectators watched the videos of eight kids the judge called "fidgeting toddlers," people seemed puzzled about why so many children had so little to say. But thanks to parents' recent reports of fresh "outcries" about being filmed at Noble's house, Kanof had a neat explanation for the kids' silence: memories of the teacher's video equipment terrorized them when they got in front of DHR's cameras.

Absent the children's voices, the parents came to the stand. As she called each one, Kanof would hand the jury enlarged color school portraits of the kids. Then the mothers and fathers would begin. Their testimony ranged from details about the sucking of breasts to stories about the licking of vaginas to tales of pencils up rectums. What they said was so devastating that the jurors almost recoiled — they would have needed nerves of steel to consider Noble's constitutional rights, much less entertain reasonable doubts about her guilt. Eric's mother, Darleen, a stylish blond Miss Texas-type, routinely began sobbing and wailing after five seconds on the stand. Other parents, including fathers, wept at every other mention of "peepee" and "boobies." Because the parents were supposed to speak for their children, they tended to use baby talk, a style soon adopted by everyone from prosecuting attorneys to the press. Any vestige of Noble's dignity disappeared as she became the cutesy and thus doubly perverse "Miss Mickey."

Before the trial began, the D.A. asked the media not to use the parents' or children's real names. Editors and station managers unquestioningly complied, but neglected to extend the same courtesy to Noble or Dove. Despite all the initial enthusiasm, a few days into the proceedings, journalists were scratching their heads. The *El Paso Times* reporter, who had a small son of his own, would come back into the newsroom every evening with a furrowed brow, moved by Noble's own children's tears and doubtful of her guilt. Staff meetings at the paper, though, focused not on such doubts or on the striking similarities between this case and McMartin, but rather on the delicate balance between how many mentions of "hiney" and "vagina" would sell papers and how many of these terms readers could stomach along with their breakfast toast.

After nine days Kanof rested her case. Noble's lawyers then spent about the same amount of time posing questions. Many of the children, for instance, had often passed Noble's and Dove's houses on their way to school or on field trips. Was it really so surprising, then, that they knew how to get to those houses from the Y? But why could they say nothing about what was inside them? And why had the police not bothered to search Noble's home to look for video cameras, or film, or receipts — or even vestiges of the children's fingerprints? Why couldn't the State produce anyone who'd ever seen two classes full of children walking near Noble's? And anyway, how could the women have walked a straggling bunch of preschoolers four blocks from the Y, undressed them, molested them, bathed them, dressed them, and walked them back again in the 90 minutes Noble was gone each time she said she'd been at the park?

Such questions were provocative, but decidedly more prosaic than Kanof's material. Noble's lawyers produced pages of charts of the Y's rather lackadaisical attendance records, trying to show that some of the children had not even been at school on the dates in February and March when the abuse was alleged to have happened. This sort of stuff was almost useless, however, because the case involved small children with hazy memories. That meant that the prosecution was allowed to present incriminating evidence dated several weeks before and after the dates mentioned in the indictment.

Noble had not even had her own class at the Y until January 1985. So the defense called a teacher named Becky, who had taught that class until then. Many children had said that they went to Mickey's house, saw her Christmas tree and ate cookies. Becky told the jury that in fact the kids had gone to *her* house, also very close to the Y, seen *her* tree and eaten cookies. Kanof countered that someone as diabolical as Noble was capable not only of molesting children right in the middle of an investigation, but was also perverse enough to set up a Christmas tree out of season just to confuse the children.

Such Machiavellian acts hardly sound like the way classical pedophiles behave. While Kanof told the jury they weren't supposed to ponder motive in figuring out if Noble had molested children, the D.A. clearly had fished around for a reason, and come up with something even worse than sexual passion — the profit motive. Before the indictments, she had told reporters Noble was connected to a "national porn ring out of Kansas."

Ironically, the only objects resembling porn in the trial were photos the defense passed around among the jurors — Polaroids of Noble's breasts. Three years earlier she had had them surgically reduced. In March 1985 she had follow-up surgery to correct scarring and returned to work, her breasts covered with fresh scars, her chest bandaged. Adults and children at the Y knew about Noble's surgery, yet the kids never mentioned seeing breast scars to their parents. Kanof recently said that at the time of the trial the children told her they'd seen "owwies" on Miss Mickey's "boobies," but she herself couldn't testify. During the trial, she remarked that it would have been just like Miss Mickey to have the surgery during the DHR's investigation, just to come up with an alibi.

Noble's attorneys brought in every witness they could think of to testify in her behalf — even Dove. To this Kanof replied that Dove had nothing to lose by appearing, since she knew she'd "go down in flames" if Noble were convicted. Besides, the D.A. told the jury, "child molesters don't have a lot of conscience…so it's pretty easy to lie."

When Noble's husband, Bill, came on the stand, Kanof had the judge dismiss the jury, then told the rest of the courtroom that Bill needed his own lawyer because he had been "positively identified" as one of the male perpetrators. When Noble's 13-year-old daughter went up to testify about her mother's spending afternoons after daycare at her junior high school, Kanof declined to cross-examine so as not to "put that child through any more than what she's going through." Though the defense could have called the Y children, the mood both in and out of the court seemed to be that such an act would be sadistic. Besides, who knew what four-year-olds might say, whether or not they'd been rehearsed? It might have been worse than their parents' testimony.

Even Ricardo the janitor came in to tell the jury he'd neither sawed open stuffed kangaroos nor engaged in more pedestrian molestations. But lost somewhere in the shuffle was Stephanie the babysitter. Only briefly mentioned during the trial, she was never called as a witness. And among all the discovery material Noble's lawyers obtained, there was no evidence that the police ever interviewed or investigated her.

The trial was the talk of the airwaves and the town, but the ten-man-two-woman jury was never sequestered. Callan twice dismissed court early so that everyone could go home and watch University of Texas at El Paso Miners basketball games on TV. Maybe the jury managed to avoid catching news broadcasts then, but it was no doubt harder to avoid glimpsing a large artist's sketch of the entire panel, including their names, occupations, and places of employment, stretched above the fold of the *El Paso Times* the morning of the second day they were deliberating their verdict.

Making their decision, weighing the defense against the State, must have been like pitting the stock pages of the *Wall Street Journal* against the Marquis de Sade — especially after Kanof used closing arguments to suddenly lower her voice and whisper that the children were probably given behavior-altering drugs and enemas. After 10 hours' deliberation, Noble was convicted on 18 of the 19 counts against her. The parents, who had played Trivial Pursuit on a court wastebasket while waiting for the verdict, said they were satisfied, and Kanof told the reporters: "I have a message to all parents: Listen to your children and love them." Next day she urged the jury to assess the maximum sentence because, "Suffer the little children and forbid them not, for of such is the kingdom of God...Michelle Noble intruded on that kingdom and twisted and perverted little children... Tell them that they will not run into her at the Safeway."

The jury did, by giving Noble life plus 311 years. Dove was later granted a change of venue to Amarillo, where she was sentenced to three life sentence plus 60 years, after a trial in which Kanof intimated that she had sex with monkeys at the zoo. A mistrial was declared after it came to light that other irregularities had occurred, including that one juror decided an appeals court would be better equipped than she to rule on Dove's case. She thought Dove was innocent but voted guilty so she wouldn't be branded as "one who condones child abuse." Then there was another trial, with another change of venue, to Lubbock. This time Dove's attorneys managed to separate her six counts so that she was tried on only one of them — sticking a pencil up a boy's rectum. Callan again presided, and several sets of parents testified, some with yet more "outcries" that the defense had never heard of, including that one boy had had a fingernail file stuffed up his anus at the Y, in front of the rest of the class. Dove got 20 years. After the sentencing, Callan proudly presented each jury member with a xeroxed copy of a sketch he'd done of them all as he sat presiding. "Was he even listening during the trial?" asked one juror, bewildered.

He wasn't the only one. The Noble/Dove affair has struck confusion — and a great unease — into El Paso. Parents are wary of daycare, community scions hesitate to sit on the boards of charitable institutions dealing with child care, teachers fear hoisting their students to the water fountain. But perhaps worst of all is the terrible sense of the world turned upside down. After all, where can we leave our kids, who is to be trusted anymore, if such acts could be committed by two ladies as pleasant as Miss Mickey and Miss Dove?

But in all this confusion one thing is clear: Noble and Dove became felons not because the assistant D.A. proved their guilt beyond a reasonable doubt, but because the women couldn't prove their innocence. They were convicted not so much by the State of Texas as by the state of hysteria sweeping the country over the problem of child molestation.

The two women were locked up hundreds of miles from El Paso, and both their families lost their savings and property to legal fees. Bill Noble and the two children have fled to another state because of Kanof's threat to indict Bill. (The D.A.'s office continued the search for the Daddy monster and the black mailman.) Noble's mother spent the summer after her conviction writing the governor, legislators, *Sixty Minutes*, lawyers chosen at random from the Yellow Pages, everyone she could think of who might be able to help open an investigation of wrongdoing by the State against her daughter.

Over a year later, she had gotten nowhere and seems bewildered. Indeed, what's poignant is the way these two women and their friends and loved ones attempt to explain what happened. A man at the zoo who tried to raise a defense fund for Dove says she should never have worked at a day-care center because people should be home taking care of their kids anyway. Noble's stepfather thinks the whole thing was a conspiracy between the D.A.'s office, the parents, and the court to get lots of money after the Y is sued. Noble, formerly an active churchgoer, thinks this is God's way of testing her, and now spends most of her free time in prison reading the Bible. Some of her more devout friends are convinced that what happened to her is part of a plan by Satan to break up happy Christian families. It seems the Devil is in this no matter who's side you're on. Dove, who was never particularly religious, told me during her last trial that "somehow I'm going to learn something from this that will serve me for the rest of my life." The look in her eyes was unnervingly rational — a look of calm anger, focused laserlike, with no heat radiating from the sides. One of her attorneys predicted Dove would get religious in prison, though. "What else can you do there to survive?" says the lawyer.

Noble's and Dove's cases were being appealed, of course, and there is a chance they will win, in which case the best that can happen is that they'll be on the street again minus their good names, their lives irretrievably disrupted. As for assistant D.A. Kanof, that isn't her job anymore. With her reputation assured after the Noble-Dove cases, she has gone on to become a federal prosecutor.

In Lubbock, during Kanof's second trial against Dove, Judge

Callan joked, "I'd like to take this show on the road all over Texas."
"How about all over the world?" Kanof laughed.

Epilogue

More than a year after Michelle Noble's trial, an appeals court ruled
that her Sixth Amendment right to confront her accusers had been
violated when the state showed the jury the videotaped interviews of
the children. She was remanded to El Paso for retrial in early 1988,
after spending more than two years behind bars.

Oddly, Noble's second trial turned into the reverse image of her
first one, largely because the hysteria that earlier gripped the community and court had finally deflated. This time around, a sober, even
contrite media did detailed treatments of the defense-related issues in
the case. And Judge Callan, who had by now read "The Making of a
Modern Witch Trial," favored the defense's motions this time even
more than he did the state's. (Noble later said that during the first trial, he had never met her eyes. Now she noticed that Callan "looked
at me like I was a human being.")

Also this time, it wasn't so much parents as children — now sev-
en and eight years old — who appeared personally to testify. But their
memories about the alleged abuse were vague, lacking, or contradictory; and their testimony was usually calm, even bemused. This time,
it was the defense, not the state, who showed the videotapes, while
the children sat next to the screen watching images of their old
preschool selves, and listening to their earlier talk of "boobies" and
"peepees" with good-humored embarrassment.

After a two-week trial, the second jury took only a few hours to
acquit Noble. A juror lambasted social workers and the police, citing
the videotapes as "tasteless" proof of how they had badgered the children. He also suggested that the Grand Jury investigate why the
D.A.'s office had ever charged Noble in the first place. Shortly afterward, the two male attorneys who tried the state's case resigned
their jobs.

Noble and her family promptly left El Paso and now live in another state. The first year of freedom was very hard for her. Emotionally traumatized and uprooted from both her old home and her long-

time prison cell, Noble nevertheless avoided seeking new friends because she didn't dare confide what happened to her to people she hardly knew. Yet the case had so drained her family financially that she couldn't afford long distance calls to El Paso. She spent her free time furiously copying Bible verses onto legal pads.

Gayle Dove's conviction was overturned several months after Noble's acquittal, and she returned to her house in an El Paso neighborhood strewn with yellow ribbons posted in her honor. Dove then spent a year with charges hanging over her while the D.A.'s office waffled on whether to retry her. A few weeks after the 1990 acquittal of Peggy McMartin Buckey, the woman defendant in the McMartin case, Dove's charges were dropped.

She vowed to stay in El Paso, her hometown. Noble says her life has slowly returned to normal. Both women say they will never again take jobs teaching children.

— *1987*

The Ritual
Sex Abuse Hoax

 The eight kids sitting in Geraldo Rivera's New York studio after the first McMartin trial ended could have stepped out of a candy bar commercial on Saturday morning TV. They gleamed with the healthy tans, shopping-mall clothes, and moussed sun-bleached hair of the southern Californian suburbs; their parents looked equally affluent. But these families were far from cheerful. "We were molested," a strapping blond teenager told the audience solemnly, "and that's an honest-to-God fact." When some of the children — most of them by now adolescents — described suffering flashbacks and night terrors, their mothers quietly dabbed at tears. Other parents seemed angry and driven. "The parents and the children standing up here will not stop," said Marymae Cioffi, who since the beginning of the case had been organizing to convince the public and the courts that bizarre sex abuse claims at places like the McMartin preschool should be believed.

As Cioffi spoke, her lips twitched in spasms of anger. The children sat politely. But when a relative of the defendants noted that the investigation had never produced any evidence against them, the eyes of a small, until then subdued 14-year-old boy suddenly turned to slits; his teeth bared and his lips trembled, just like Cioffi's. For even though the jury had completely exonerated Peggy McMartin Buckey while acquitting her son Ray on most counts and deadlocking on the rest, Geraldo's guests insisted their former teachers really were sadistic sex criminals.

Geraldo reminded the audience that defendants are innocent until proved guilty. But he also asked whether the acquittals spelled doom for future child abuse prosecutions, and titled the program "The McMartin Outrage: What Went Wrong?" Finally, when he patted the children's shoulders and remarked on their "sincere pain," it was clear this show was adding to the pressures that would lead to the current retrial of Ray Buckey on eight hung counts involving three girls.

What Geraldo neglected to mention was that none of these children had ever taken the stand: since McMartin first hit the media in 1984, his guests' accusations had been so consistently bizarre and illogical that their testimony would only have damaged the case. There was 18-year-old Chris Collins, whose father belongs to a McMartin parents' group that believes the teachers are part of an international Satanic conspiracy. Collins, who insists he was molested attending McMartin in the mid-'70s, remembers a room below the school office and "major, major sacrifices" connected with the "Satanic Church." The problem with his claim is that when Collins was at McMartin, Ray Buckey was in high school and, according to his mother, maintained a perfect attendance record — meaning he was never at the preschool when Collins was. Then there was round-faced, 10-year-old Elizabeth Cioffi. According to her father, she has talked about being molested under the school in tunnels lined with flashing lights and pictures of the devil.

Irrationality pervaded the McMartin case from the beginning. The first allegation came from a woman later diagnosed as a paranoid schizophrenic. After Judy Johnson noticed one day in 1983 that her two-year-old son's bottom was red, she told police he said something about a man named Ray at his nursery school. In the next few weeks, Johnson accused 25-year-old Buckey of donning a mask and sodomizing her child while sticking his head in a toilet; of wearing a cape while taping the boy's mouth, hands, and eyes; and of sticking an air tube in his rectum. She also said Ray made the child ride naked on a horse and molested him while dressed as a cop, fireman, clown, and Santa Claus. Later, she claimed that McMartin teachers, including Ray's 57-year-old mother, Peggy, jabbed scissors into the boy's eyes and staples in his ears, nipples, and tongue; that Ray put her son's finger into a goat's anus; and that Peggy killed a baby and made the boy drink the blood. She also told the D.A.'s office that an AWOL marine and three models in a health club had raped her son, and that the family dog was sodomized as well.

Within a few months, Peggy, Ray, his 28-year-old sister, his 77-year-old wheelchair bound grandmother, and three other women teachers would be jailed and charged with hundreds of counts of sex abuse. During the investigation, some parents would claim that hundreds of Los Angeles-area children were brutally molested in several day-care centers, over a 20-year period, by a conspiracy of Satanic child pornographers. Children would talk about playing the "Naked Movie Star" game, about being photographed nude, about sexual assault in hot-air balloons, on faraway farms, on the shoulders of busy highways, in cemeteries, in tunnels under the school yard.

The McMartin school was painstakingly probed for tunnels. None were found. Neither was child pornography, nor witnesses from the traffic-filled freeways, nor any other evidence. Doctors' findings of physical signs of abuse were later debunked by medical researchers. Child protection experts have since criticized the prosecution's social workers for using leading, suggestive interviewing methods that resembled brainwashing. Judy Johnson was hospitalized for psychosis in early 1985 (she later died of an alcoholism-related liver disease). An assistant D.A. who quit the case and then helped the defense told the press over three years ago that the woman had been mentally ill when she made her first charges — information the McMartin jurors were never allowed to hear.

But none of these revelations seemed to dampen the prosecutors', the media's, or the public's need to believe horrible things had happened at McMartin. For the first two years, the press slavishly trumpeted every illogical accusation, so that when charges against five women defendants were dropped in 1986 — after the Los Angeles D.A. called the evidence "incredibly weak" — polls showed that most people still thought abuse had occurred at the pre-school. During the subsequent, almost three-year trial, neither the *Los Angeles Times* nor the rest of the metropolitan media bothered to critically dissect the case.

Finally the verdicts were announced, but the fact that they were overwhelmingly not guilty didn't seem to matter either. In each of the 13 hung decisions, from 7 to 11 jurors decided in Buckey's favor, but this was glossed over by the press. So were the comments of jurors like Darryl Hutchins: he said that during deliberations he decided Ray Buckey had molested the first child, but that he would have voted differently had the judge allowed testimony about the mother's mental illness — or the defense's contention that while the McMartin defendants were in jail, the little boy was molested by his father.

Refiling counts that most of the jury has rejected is almost unheard of. Immediately after the verdicts, however, McMartin parents began a media campaign to push the D.A. to prosecute Ray Buckey a second time. Again, the press dealt uncritically with the pressure. On tabloids like *Geraldo* and *Oprah*, support for a retrial was overt; "responsible" media like *The New York Times* were more subtle, suggesting, for example, that the jurors in the first trial were "stymied" by "the malleable memories of children and the distorting effects of questioning, particularly when a child has been traumatized." Hardly anyone acknowledged that most of the jurors had concluded the children had likely not been abused, except possibly by their own relatives and certainly by the investigation itself.

Clearly, the public had come to believe that something as monstrous-sounding, yet as patently absurd, as McMartin was eminently imaginable. So imaginable in fact that a rash of similar cases surfaced across the country. A month after the McMartin investigation started, a Jordan, Minnesota, garbage collector accused of molesting three girls told authorities several local families were in a child sex ring. The charges against the middle-aged couples met widespread disbelief. But as neighbors stepped forward to support the accused, they, too, were arrested — the children had named them as perpetrators. Stories of ritual and slaughter emerged after the children were removed to foster care and many were interviewed more than 30 times apiece. The murder tales were later deemed fabrications, and some children admitted they'd lied to get relentless interviewers to leave them in peace. A husband and wife were acquitted, charges against 21 others were dropped, and the garbage collector confessed to inventing the charges in hopes of getting a lighter sentence.

In Chicago, a child told her mother that a day-care janitor had tickled her vagina. During repeated interviews, some 300 others children accused 40 teachers of abusing them during Satanic rituals, complete with baby-killing. No physical evidence was produced; the janitor was tried anyway and acquitted. Several other cases surfaced, and by 1985, McMartin parents with media connections were collaborating with ABC's "20/20" on shows claiming that "Satanic" crime and day-care abuse were epidemic. Other journalists ran with the story, disregarding the lack of evidence. Meanwhile, prosecutors, police, and social workers were attending nationwide conferences to "net-work" with "experts" on Satanic kiddie porn conspiracies and learn how to root them out of nursery schools. There was a wave of cases that year, among them one in El Paso, Texas, where two women teachers were accused. Investigators were in touch with McMartin child interviewers and with Satanic Conspiracy theorist Ken Wooden, who helped produce the "20/20" series. The preschoolers never testified; instead, parents described their children's "outcries" since the investigation had started, and behavioral changes like masturbating, urinating on walls, and assuming "sexual" postures. The teachers were convicted.

In these and some thirty others covered by the Memphis, Tennessee *Commercial Appeal* in a 1988 series, journalists noted striking similarities in what child protection officials dubbed "ritual abuse" cases. Investigations usually began because of vague medical symptoms or after an upper-middle-class child did something that adults thought inappropriately sexual. Then, even though most sexual abuse occurs within the family, investigators immediately directed their inquiries outside the home. Sometimes they even suspected community sex rings, but most often they focused on elite childcare centers. The first allegation sometimes seemed plausible. But in remarkable departures from forensics, police, social workers, doctors, and therapists badgered children to name more victims and perpetrators, ignoring answers that contradicted a ritual abuse scenario. As a result, many men were charged; but women were too, and this was especially shocking, since females have not been thought of as child molesters, much less sex torturers.

From 1984 to 1989, some 100 people nationwide were charged with ritual sex abuse; of those, 50 or so were tried and about half convicted, with no evidence but testimony from children, parents, "experts" expounding on how the children acted traumatized, and doctors talking about tiny white lines on anuses or bumps on hymens — "signs of abuse" that later research would show on nonabused children. By 1986, in many states, hastily reformed criminal statutes made it unnecessary for children to come into court; parents could act as hearsay witness, or kids could testify on closed-circuit TV, giving juries the automatic impression the defendants had done something to frighten the child. And once a person stood accused, the community often decided that *something* must have happened. Any remaining skeptics were blasted for "condoning child abuse" and some were accused themselves.

As the cases snowballed, many parents were skeptical, but therapists told doubters that unless they believed the allegations, their children would be further traumatized. Anxious, guilt-ridden parents formed organizations with names like Believe the Children, the group begun by McMartin parents. Besides offering psychological support, these groups helped prosecutors put together cases, did media promotion, and lobbied for laws such as those allowing children to testify outside the courtroom.

Despite the support they received from adults, instead of getting calmer as time passed, many of the children showed increasingly traumatized behavior, such as flashbacks. Their tales of abuse followed a pattern; at first they said they were merely fondled; later in the investigation, they mentioned rape, sodomy, and pornography; then they progressed to increasingly bizarre scenarios. Across the country, the molesters were described as black men, mulattos, deformed people, or clowns; the abuse took place in churches; adults wore masks and costumes; they urinated and defecated on children; they burned, stabbed, cooked, or drowned babies; they sacrificed animals; they molested children in funeral homes and buried Barbie dolls. Extensive investigations have failed to turn up material evidence to support any of these claims.

In a 1987 case in Holland, the authorities decided there were no culprits at all. A four-year-old boy in the town of Oude Pekkela returned home from a play area with a bloody anus. In the next few months, some 100 children told authorities that German pornographers dressed as clowns had kidnapped, molested, and tortured them in Satanic rituals, and as time passed they acted more and more traumatized. But after a massive investigation, officials concluded that the four-year-old had poked himself with twigs while playing with another preschooler; that no German pornographers — or any other molesters — had ever existed. And in suburban Philadelphia, where an investigation began last year into claims that a teacher and her 68-year old aide ritually assaulted three girls with excrement, the Bucks County D.A. dismissed the allegations as hysteria. Still, an unquestioning belief in ritual sex abuse in the U.S., Canada, and other postindustrial countries remains the rule. Here, not only religious fundamentalists and the unschooled, but large numbers of literate, secular people seem ready to accept the idea that scores of people in crowded daycare centers could engage hundreds of children in vicious — not to say extremely messy — assaults, and yet leave neither a scintilla of physical evidence nor an adult material witness. What's going on?

In a sense, nothing new. Moral panics — the Salem witch trials and McCarthyism, for example — have often run rampant through cultures in flux, and "ritual abuse" is today's mythic expression of deep-seated worries over sweeping changes in the family. Since the 1970s, the number of working women have risen, and so have the divorce rates and female-headed households. Children are being socialized less by family authority and more by the media and its consumerist focus on the erotic, yet AIDS has imbued eros with a new danger. All these changes spell anxiety. For conservatives, they are literally sinful, and since moral traditionalists hate public day-care, a right-wing impulse to demonize childcare workers is not surprising. But many feminist and progressives have bought into the hysteria, too: ritual abuse panic has become an outlet for women's rage at sexual violence and harassment. While this anger could hardly be more justified, it has increasingly been articulated through an anti-sexual current in the feminist movement, a current that jibes with the views of conservatives who loathe pornography — and who also fear women, their need for day-care, their independence, and their sexuality.

Until recently, generations of silence and denial shrouded the problem of child sexual abuse, especially incest. Academic literature had long described it as a one-in-a-million event, and when women and girls told therapists and child protection authorities they had been molested, their stories were usually dismissed as nasty figments of the female psyche. But by the mid-70s, as feminists were fighting this society's tendency to belittle and disbelieve women's rape reports, theoreticians like Florence Rush began eloquently arguing that children — especially girls — had the same problem when they tried to talk about being sexually abused. Meanwhile, several studies reported that one of every hundred women remembered having sex with fathers and stepfathers — and that did not even include experiences with other family members like uncles. By 1980, thanks largely to feminist efforts to create and publicize reporting systems, the government tallied almost 43,000 cases of sex abuse annually, up from a few thousand only a few years earlier. Most perpetrators were fathers and other male relatives and most of the victims were girls.

Feminists who analyzed incest defined it as inherently victimizing the daughter; they said her extreme dependence on her family and the men in it meant she could not give meaningful consent to sex. But then they made a dubious leap: they began applying their perspective on incest to non-relatives. Judith Herman, in her 1982 book, *Father-Daughter Incest*, wrote that any sexual relationship between an adult and a child, even if the child is a teenager, "must necessarily take on some of the coercive characteristics of rape." Florence Rush compared children choosing adult sex partners to chickens meeting up with hungry foxes.

Actually, studies show that the realities of transgenerational sex outside the family, where individual adults wield a good deal less power over children, are more ambiguous. Most male pedophilia consists of caressing and fondling. For most children, these experiences appear to be at best confusing, at worst traumatic. But others seem to willingly participate, and some adults recall that while still legally minors they accepted, even welcomed sex with grownups. (Many gay men, for example, say they instigated these encounters, and some suggest that such relationships offer the boys the only real possibility for healthy acculturation into homosexuality.) Nonetheless, the prevailing feminist view of child sexual abuse broadened its meaning to include, without distinctions, any contract between someone below the age of consent with someone older — even if that meant ignoring how the younger partner remembered the incident.

In the early 1980s, feminist sociologist Diana Russell asked women to remember any unwanted sexual contact before age 18, including with boyfriends of the same age — "sexual contact meaning anything from anal intercourse to glimpsing a flasher to an unwelcome hug." She also asked women to recall "incest," defined as sexual contact between relatives (even distant ones) more than five years apart in age. By Russell's standards, tongue kissing between a 13-year-old and her cousin's 19-year-old husband would be considered incestuous and therefore exploitative, even if the woman remembered enjoying it. Using her extravagantly broad definitions, she found that one in five women are "incest victims" and more than half have suffered child sexual abuse. Because the media quoted this and similar studies without explaining how diverse the reported experiences were, it suddenly seemed to the public that little kids were in imminent danger of being raped.

But even before feminist anti-sex abuse efforts had begun, a national fear was growing that terrible, previously unheard of perversities were endangering children. It began with rumors of Halloween sadists. In 1970, *The New York Times* reported that the "plump red apple that Junior gets from a kindly old woman down the block...may have a razor blade hidden inside." By 1972, many kids were not allowed to trick-or-treat; three years later *Newsweek* warned that several children were dead and hundreds more injured by viciously doctored Halloween candy. A few years later, kiddie porn was the new threat. In 1977, NBC reported that "as many as two million American youngsters are involved in the fast-growing, multi-million dollar child pornography business..." and "police say the number of boy prostitutes may be as high as a million" (some 10 percent of all male adolescents in the entire country).

Then, in the early 1980s, following the New York City disappearance of Etan Patz, the kidnapping and slaying of Adam Walsh, and the murders of 28 Atlanta schoolchildren, the missing children's movement emerged. Crusaders began describing a stranger abduction problem of astonishing proportions: U.S. Representative Paul Simon offered House members a "conservative estimate... 50,000 children abducted by strangers annually," and a leading child-search organization said 5000 of these children were murdered each year.

Research by journalists and sociologists has debunked all these claims. In the entire U.S., only one child has ever been killed by Halloween candy — and the poison was put out there by his own father. Only 18 injuries were reported nationwide during the 25 years before 1984, the most serious one a wound requiring some stitches. Some of these were hoaxes or fabrications by attention-seeking kids. As for kiddie porn, it's estimated that even before 1978, when all production and commercial distribution of such material was banned under federal law, only about 5000 and 7000 children were involved worldwide. Since then the commercial market in America, minuscule to begin with, has been virtually wiped out.

Research into claims about mass kidnappings likewise deflates the hype: a recently released Justice Department study finds that almost all missing children are teenage runaways or throwaways. The typical kidnapping is committed by a divorced parent who has lost custody. As for stranger-abductions, the Washington, D.C.-based National Center for Missing and Exploited Children currently lists about 240 children missing in the entire country. Still, much of the American public is convinced that molesters, sadists, kidnappers, and pornographers are major threats to our kids.

This fear has been reinforced by yet another strand of irrationality — the rise of paranoia about Satanism. Religious belief in child-torturing conspiracies of devil worshipers — whether Christian, Jewish, or Satanist — has flowered and withered since the early days of the Church. Lately, the belief has resurged in the U.S. and gained widespread acceptance via tabloid media like *Geraldo*. Things have gotten so out of hand that last year a Texas school district told students they could no longer wear T-shirts with peace symbols, since self-styled experts on Satanism say the design represents the devil. Another popular belief, that Satanists kidnap blonde virgins for sacrifice, cropped up nationwide in 1987 and 1988, and spawned a wave of what sociologist Jeffrey Victor calls "rumor panics": townspeople from Montana to Maine banned library books, armed themselves into vigilante squads, and raided purported "covens" that often turned out to be nothing more than teen punk-rocker hangouts.

The latest Satan scare has its roots in 1970s fundamentalism. In *The Late Great Planet Earth* and *Satan is Alive and Well on Planet Earth*, both of which sold millions of copies, Christian TV celebrity Hal Lindsey decries the corrupting influence of the "New Age" '60s, yearningly prophesies the end of the world and Armageddon, and warns of the sinister power of rock music, witches and devil worshipers. Meanwhile, many white teenagers shocked their elders by reading popular works about Satanism, scrawling "666"-style graffiti, and listening to the music Cardinal O'Connor, in his recent "exorcism" sermon, called pornography in sound.

During the late '70s, "urban legends," or modern folk rumors, about devil worshipers spread across the U.S. One tale had it that Ray Kroc, former owner of McDonald's, had tithed his hamburger profits to the church of Satan in exchange for prosperous Big Mac sales. Another was that Procter & Gamble's century-old moon-and-stars logo was a secret Satanic symbol. (The rumor got so out of control that the company had to change the logo in 1985.)

Another evolution in the populist zeitgeist was signaled by the 1980 release of *Michelle Remembers*, coauthored by Lawrence Pazder, a Catholic psychiatrist from Vancouver, and his wife and former patient, Michelle Smith. The book recounts how Smith, in treatment for depression, underwent months of hypnosis and "remembered" being imprisoned at age five by her mother and a group of Satanists. She said she was locked up, buried with snakes, smeared with human waste, raped with candles and crucifixes, and finally forced to destroy an infant. Smith's therapy consisted of more hypnosis, prayers to the Virgin Mary, and exorcism.

There is no confirmation that anything Smith "remembers" occurred. Psychiatric anthropologist Sherrill Mulhern, who has reviewed tapes of sessions similar to Pazder's and Smith's, says patients retain an unshakable belief in whatever a therapist suggests under hypnosis. Smith's "memories," Mulhern says, were probably constructed piecemeal, with Pazder introducing the Satanic motifs. Still, *Michelle Remembers* became a "non-fiction" bestseller, and the authors appeared on national Christian talk shows. Another self-styled cult survivor had her story published in a tabloid, and by 1983 the FBI was getting calls from women around the country, claiming they too had escaped devil-worshiping cults. Their stories hardly varied: the cults were part of a generations-old, international conspiracy including prominent people, and practiced rites like the ones in *Michelle Remembers*; they also kidnapped and sacrificed children, which explained the country's thousands of missing kids.

According to Kenneth Lanning of the FBI, at first the agency took the stories seriously. Perhaps there were a few isolated cults, maybe they could have killed some children. Authorities nationwide began digging up reported burial sites, but found nothing, and Lanning's doubts increased as "survivor" reports mushroomed (the FBI now gets a call a day). "If the cults were real," he says, "they would constitute the greatest conspiracy in history."

Who, then, are these "survivors" and what's their connection to ritual abuse accusations? Sherrill Mulhern, who has spent years studying traditional cults and modern groups like Jonestown, began researching the "survivors" and their therapists about five years ago. She soon realized she was looking not at a real cult, but at people linked by a delusionary belief in one.

Many "survivors," Mulhern says, are former teen runaways who lived on the streets and took up prostitution — behavior typical of incest victims. Many have abused drugs that produce paranoid delusions; many have been treated for schizophrenia and for borderline personality, which is characterized by compulsive lying. More recently, many have been diagnosed by therapists as suffering from multiple personality disorder. And virtually all had fundamentalist Christian parents or later converted. While being "born again," they were often hypnotized by fellow "survivors" or by self-styled Christian spiritual therapists.

The public knows about multiple personality from *The Three Faces of Eve* and *Sybil*. This diagnosis — which was called double consciousness in the 19th century and later fell out of favor — has been officially resurrected during the past 15 years by the American psychiatric profession. A century ago, Freud's term for multiple personality was hysteria, and he first treated hysterical women during the 1880s. When hypnotizing deeply religious Catholic patients, Freud was struck by how many told trance tales of being raped by black-robed Satan worshipers, stories identical to those told by women during earlier witch trials. He speculated that these stories were actually sadomasochistic fantasies overlying memories of real childhood incest but articulated in the language of religion.

A century later, therapists started hearing the same tales again. This time around, they weren't so willing to call them fictions. The new, unqualified belief that all women's and girls' rape and incest stories were true reflected the reemergence of that strain in feminist thinking that condemned all sexual impulses as merely forms of male domination. In this view, men were inherently predatory, obsessed with penetration and violence — or, as Andrea Dworkin put it, "the stuff of murder, not love." Women, on the other hand, wanted gentle, not-necessarily-even-genital-sex. By analogy, children were just as pure.

Feminists like Diana Russell, Florence Rush, and Dworkin denied that sadomasochistic acts or thoughts could be erotic for women. Russell viewed them as inventions of the patriarch and reflections of women's powerlessness; Rush, in her groundbreaking work on sex abuse, *The Best Kept Secret*, disapprovingly connected the "uncensored erotic imagination" with the "total freedom of the sadist." Besides being theoreticians, these women were also activists in Women Against Pornography, which was lending the right's anti-porn crusade a modern "progressive" aura by arguing, despite the lack of evidence, that representations of women being wounded or sexually dominated by men cause sexual violence. At the same time, many therapists who considered themselves feminists adopted the belief that when patients bring up fantasies, dreams, or memories of coerced or brutal sex, these can never be products of the erotic imagination; they must really have happened — and anyone who says otherwise is an apologist for patriarchal violence.

That was the complaint lodged against Freud. During his early career, when female hysterics told him they had been seduced during childhood by their fathers and other adults, Freud believed them; he concluded such violations were common and led to neurosis. Later, he decided many of the stories were untrue. Freud undoubtedly ended up underestimating the prevalence of abuse, though he never dismissed all his patients' seduction stories. To explain the others as fantasies, he developed the theory of the Oedipus complex.

In recognizing children as intensely sexual beings, the theory was revolutionary. But its assumption that all women envy men their penises helped reinforce sexual stereotypes and encouraged therapists to mindlessly dismiss women's memories of childhood molestation. Not surprisingly, then, Freud's theories of sexuality were later just as simplistically attacked by feminists eager to conflate sexuality with male violence. Their criticisms were most forcefully articulated in 1984, with the publication of Jeffrey Masson's *The Assault on Truth: Freud's Suppression of the Seduction Theory*.

And even as Masson institutionalized Freud-bashing, women and children were telling therapists and police rococo tales about sadomasochistic, diabolical assaults. How could these bizarre stories be true? But then, hadn't we learned that sex abuse was much more common than previously thought?

The stage was set for McMartin hysteria.

In 1983, as part of his upcoming, hotly contested reelection campaign, the Los Angeles district attorney commissioned a survey asking voters to name their biggest crime concerns. He was surprised to discover that their main worry wasn't drugs or drunken driving — it was child abuse. At about the same time the pollsters were at work, a mentally ill mother was telling Los Angeles County authorities *Story-of-O* tales about the McMartin preschool. Following her first accusations, police sent 200 letters to parents, listing specific questions to ask their children about whether and how Ray Buckey molested them. Virtually all the children denied being abused. Nevertheless, at the suggestion of the prosecution, panicked families made appointments at the Children's Institute International (CII), a Los Angeles abuse therapy clinic.

There, social workers plied the children with puppets, suggested ritual abuse scenarios, coaxed recalcitrant kids to "pretend," and said if they didn't tell the "yucky secret" it meant they were stupid. This interviewing method followed from Los Angeles psychiatrist Roland Summit's "child sexual abuse accommodation syndrome," a theory about incest. Summit argues that if there is evidence of sex abuse and a child denies it, this is only further proof that it happened and a therapist should use any means necessary to help the child talk. When this technique was applied to criminal investigation, there wasn't supposed to be any problem with false allegations. Research has since suggested that as many as one in twelve sex abuse reports are fabricated, that in divorce custody disputes, the rate may be as high as one in two, and that a disturbingly common source of false allegations is mentally ill mothers who injure their children, even genitally, to get attention. But in 1984, few were thinking about such issues — conventional wisdom was that since children are innocent beings, they never lie about sexual abuse. If they later recant, that means they are under family pressure to protect the father — and their turnabout is further proof of the crime.

So no matter how much coercion was used to get an accusation and no matter if a child later retracted it, once Summit's incest theory was applied, a charge of abuse became irrefutable. Child protection workers ignored the fact that this logic had little to do with day-care. After all, why would children staunchly deny abuse to protect an adult who wasn't part of the family? And if they'd been so brutally attacked at school, why wouldn't they tell their parents?

Therapists and investigators came up with all sorts of rationales. One was that the teachers threatened them by slaughtering animals and warning that the same thing would happen to their parents if they told. Kids who revealed nothing were said to have split off unbearable memories and developed amnesia. Following this line of thinking, it's not surprising that some investigators and psychologists used hypnotic suggestion to get children to "remember" abuse; more typical was endless interrogation, much of it done by parents.

In imposing such techniques, adults no doubt injected their own motifs into allegations. Indeed, there is evidence that the details in ritual abuse charges come more from grown-ups than children. Lawrence Pazder, coauthor of *Michelle Remembers,* told the *San Francisco Examiner* he acted as a consultant to Los Angeles police investigating McMartin and to parents nationwide; McMartin parent Jackie McGaulley has confided she met with him during the early days of the investigation. Around the same time, Ken Wooden, the Satanic conspiracy theorist, mailed information to 3,500 prosecutors describing what to look for in ritual abuse cases. Women claiming to be survivors contacted McMartin investigators and parents; some even joined parents at nationwide child protection conferences to speak about ritual abuse. Meanwhile, prominent psychiatrists like Bennett Braun began appearing at symposia on multiple personality, telling colleagues that a fourth of the women with this diagnosis are escapees from cults organized like the "Communist cell structure." Soon, other therapists would be carrying guns for protection against devil worshipers. And soon, more and more prosecutors would make front-page news by leveling charges of unspeakably sadistic rape, sodomy and terrorism against people whose only previous experience with the law was in traffic court.

Yet Satanism as a motive in ritual abuse cases didn't always wash: Though prosecutors tried to keep it quiet, if the public or jury found out that the accusations included the belief that the defendants danced around in covens, cases tended to become laughingstocks and collapse. (Indeed, the phrase *ritual abuse* was coined by child protection people worried that *Satanic abuse* would evoke public disbelief.) So prosecution-minded child-protection activists tried to develop sensible-sounding explanations for why ordinary people would suddenly get the urge to stick swords up toddlers.

To do this, common sense had to be reformed. Nobody, not even the most jaded of cops, had ever heard of people with no relationship to enragé politics or cults and with no mental health problems practicing intricate sexual tortures against little children in nursery schools. The situation was akin to the dilemma faced by inquisitors during the witch trials, when one of the biggest issues was how to *physically* identify a consort of Satan. The accused would be stripped and a search would ensue for "devil's privy marks": warts, scars, and skin tags, especially on the genitals. Such blemishes were said to prove the bearer had a compact with the devil. Three hundred years later, bodily flaws wouldn't do. Now what was needed was a new psychology.

Serious research was no help. Most male molesters and pedophiles who commit non-violent offenses score normally on psychological tests, but one would expect a Rorschach to ferret out something remarkable about a person who rubs feces on toddlers and barbecues babies. Nevertheless, batteries of exams given to ritual abuse defendants turned up virtually nothing unusual. This was especially remarkable when it came to women, since the few female child molesters mentioned in earlier medical literature had invariably been diagnosed as mentally retarded or psychotic.

But in the 1980s, rapidly increasing reports of incest included several cases with female perpetrators. Recent studies suggest that these women are usually emotionally disturbed, abuse drugs, and were themselves incest victims. When molesting their children, they do it nonviolently, by fondling them during diaper changes, for example; and they often feel ashamed and turn themselves in. Others report helping their husbands molest their daughters. These women seem to share many traits with battered wives, and after escaping abusive marriages, some have willingly confessed their former complicity.

As soon as female incest offender studies were published in the mid-1980s, prosecutors of ritual cases rushed to pound the accused into the profiles. In most cases, it takes a huge stretch of the imagination to link ritual defendants with incest offenders. The former don't have drug or mental health problems. Accused groups have usually contained more women than men, and that doesn't fit the battered or dominated wife profiles. And virtually all the defendants have insisted they are innocent even after generous plea bargaining.

Nevertheless, zealous child protection authorities keep trying to suggest "profiles," even if it means fictionalizing defendants' lives. In several cases, with no supporting evidence, officials have told journalists that the accused were "abused as children." In others, prosecutors have intimated that benign activities, often having something to do with sex, reflect psychopathology. In one case, a middle-aged married woman had an affair (with a man) while she was working at a preschool; one week, when she was considering leaving her husband, she signed the daily attendance sheet with her maiden name. At trial, the prosecutor displayed the signatures and implied the woman was mentally ill.

Another profile gained popularity after the 1985 Meese Commission hearing where critics of adult pornography were joined by spokespeople for the kiddie porn, missing children, and ritual abuse panics. Appearing with a chart supposedly describing confessed and convicted male sex abusers, the FBI's Lanning advised cops to check whether a suspect seemed Regressed ("low self-esteem"); Inadequate ("social misfit"); Morally Indiscriminate ("a user and abuser of people"); Sexually Indiscriminate ("try-sexual — willing to try anything"). Though this typology is about as scientific as a horoscope, Lanning, a vocal Satanic-conspiracy-theory skeptic, has cautioned that his chart wasn't developed for women or ritual abuse defendants — which hasn't kept prosecutors from using it.

Even so, the search for a more convincing profile goes on. In response to true believers' urgings, the federal government followed Meese Commission recommendations and funded studies that accept, a priori, the validity of ritual abuse charges. In 1985, the University of California at Los Angeles got $450,000 to monitor into adulthood the "coping" skills of children allegedly molested in local preschools, though authorities later dismissed virtually all their stories as unbelievable.

One researcher for this study is sociologist David Finkelhor, a self-styled sexual progressive and longtime colleague of feminist Diana Russell. Finkelhor got a grant to profile day-care sex crimes. Again, most of the cases he researched had so many investigative and evidentiary flaws that they never made it to trial. Except for idle speculations, Finkelhor found nothing remarkable in ritual defendants' histories or personalities. But instead of asking if this meant the charges were false, he implied that since the accused are normal, being normal is part of the typology of the ritual offender. With this sleight of hand, the study, titled *Nursery Crimes*, immediately became a bible for child protection fanatics eager to supply incredulous communities and journalists with a "scientific" rationale for their paranoia.

The updating of ritual abuse hysteria with pop psychology is vividly illustrated in New Jersey's Margaret Kelly Michaels case — the northeast's version of McMartin. Michaels, a teacher at a suburban Newark day-care center, was accused in 1985 of assaulting preschoolers sexually with peanut butter, swords, bloodied tampons, urine, feces, and terroristic threats. She was said to have committed these crimes against dozens of children daily, for seven months, in a crowded facility, without any adults seeing her and without leaving any physical evidence.

After investigators made all the mistakes that characterized

McMartin, they still had no evidence that Michaels was in a cult. So they searched for psychopathology. Again, nothing strange in Michaels' background. They pressed on anyway. To fit her into the incest offender profile, prosecutors played up unfounded rumors that her father fondled her during jailhouse visits. At a preliminary hearing, they brought in the FBI's Lanning to "instruct" the judge that women don't have to be psychotic to molest children. Both in court and off the record, the prosecutors plugged Michaels into anything that passed for a profile, even those developed for men. They suggested she was "dissociated" — i.e., a multiple personality — because she did dance exercises at the day-care center while looking "spacey." They implied she was a pedophile — a term never before applied to women — because she took photographs at the playground. And the fact that Michaels adamantly insisted she was innocent was supposed to mean she was "morally indiscriminate." As proof of her cunning, prosecutors told the jury that during one psychological evaluation, Michaels drew a person with one foot turned inward; but another time she drew it pointed out!

With such nonsense offered — and largely accepted — as "motive," it was unavoidable that Michaels would be demonized for any sexual behavior not conforming to the strictest traditional standards. At her women's college, for example, she had experimented with lesbianism. The prosecution insinuated that Michael's homosexual experiences and the fact that she had not slept with a man until age 25, were proof of "confusion" that would cause her to torture children. Michaels was ultimately convicted on 115 counts of abuse. The case against her, permeated as it was by the testimony of social workers and psychologists, exchanged open talk of Satanic conspiracies for a secular, feminist-sounding idiom that nevertheless couches a profound hostility towards women and a loathing for any erotic impulse.

Even children's play with each other is becoming suspect. Abuse-finders now worry that preschoolers who play sexually with their peers may be "perpetrators" or pedophiles-in-the-making. CII, the Los Angeles clinic known for its abominable McMartin interviews, is now treating "offenders" as young as four years old if they have so much as "verbally cajoled" a younger child into sex play that CII deems not "normal." While researchers say most of the "offenders" were themselves sexually abused, the clinic's history of eliciting false allegations makes any such claims suspect. More telling is the CII therapists' disapproval that some of their little girl patients said they acted sexually not out of "love or caring," but simply to "feel good."

While such rhetoric may still be patently laughable, repressing older kids is another story. Teenagers are increasingly victimized by laws denying them access to birth control, confidential abortions, or a sense that sex is anything more than a deadly disease. The trend is now justified via the rhetoric of "child protection": in Arizona, after a law passed mandating teachers and counselors to report sex abuse victims, officials in the state's largest school district gathered the names of sexually active students and handed them over to the cops.

Meanwhile, in divorce disputes and especially on the day-care front, hysteria continues unabated. Across the country, more and more losers in custody battles are accusing spouses of being Satanic cult sex abusers. And since 1989, the town of Edenton, North Carolina, has been disrupted by charges that five women and two men associated with an elite preschool molested, raped, and filmed sex acts with 70 young children and infants. Earlier in the investigation, officials said they had hard photographic evidence of the crimes, and the D.A. claims the children have made most of their accusations to therapists. But the only "evidence" to emerge is one Polaroid photo, found in a woman defendant's home, of her having sex with her fiancé (an adult); at least one therapist is giving Satanism and ritual abuse seminars around the state, and some parents of the alleged victims are active in Believe the Children.

The North Carolina kids' stories have unerringly followed the ritual abuse plot, progressing lately to tales of witnessing babies slaughtered. Perhaps not coincidentally, their most bizarre allegations began surfacing this past fall, around the time that 27 million television viewers watched Do You Know the Muffin Man?, a CBS movie that rehashed details from several ritual cases, but included the wholly fictional climax of parents discovering day-care teachers worshiping the devil amidst piles of kiddie porn. Or maybe the North Carolina children saw an earlier Oprah Winfrey show in which a Jewish woman, accompanied by her Jewish therapist, claimed to be a survivor of childhood cult ritual abuse and added that Jewish families had been sacrificing babies since the 1700s.

A few months later, during the taping of the Geraldo post-trial show, the McMartin children and their parents sat under bright lights and gave their names. Back at a Los Angeles studio hookup, a girl sat in a darkened area, anonymous. She told how when she was five she used to spend after-school hours with Ray Buckey, helping him clean up classrooms, yet he never molested her. She recalled going to CII during the investigation, and how the therapists there kept suggesting the details of ritual sex games before they even started up the tape recorder. Then they turned it on, all the while telling her things she'd never heard of, and insisting she repeat them.

She wouldn't, and now, six years later, a boy sitting in the bright lights — one whose parents parade him on national TV and make speeches about Satanist sex abuse networks in Episcopal churches — glared at her silhouette and insisted she was really molested. The girl sat in the shadows, afraid to show her face or give her name. She and her family fear harassment — not for proclaiming she was raped, but for insisting she wasn't.

As for the children who sat in the light, their parents have invested years believing in demonic conspiracies and underground nursery tunnels. (Until recently, the parents were still digging. They came up with Indian artifacts.) They have spoken unremittingly of such things, to the world and to their sons and daughters. They have told their children, over and over, that they were abused, then rewarded them for acting traumatized. They have put them in therapy with adult fanatics who have done the same, and enrolled them as guinea pigs in the "research" projects of zealots.

The McMartin kids, and hundreds of others in ritual abuse spin-offs across the country, have spent years trapped in clans now extended to include psychologists, social workers and prosecutors — clans whose identity derives from a tent-revival belief in their children's imagined victimization. Right wing devil-mongers may find this subculture to their liking, but the rest of us ought to recognize the harm it is wreaking, not only on civil liberties and the falsely accused, but also on day-care, on women's rights, and especially on children. Because the kids involved in this hysteria have indeed suffered, but not at the hands of their teachers. And the abuses perpetrated against them by a child-protection movement gone mad are every bit as awful as the tyranny of incest.

— *1990*

DEBBIE NATHAN, formerly a reporter for the *El Paso Times*, is a regular contributor to *The Village Voice*, *The Chicago Reader*, *The Texas Observer* and other journals of culture and politics. In 1988 she received the H.L. Mencken Award for Investigative Journalism for her article "The Making of a Modern Witch Trial."